The 7 Secrets of Appalachian Folk Magic

HOW TO HARNESS MOUNTAIN MAGIC & TRADITIONAL ROOTWORK FOR PROTECTION, HEALING, AND ANCESTRAL CONNECTION

MADAME OPHELIA

First Edition: 2026

Table of Content

Introduction

Imagine standing at the threshold of a world where the spells you've learned, the remedies you've brewed, and the protective charms you've painstakingly crafted are not just rote actions but vibrant expressions of genuine power. Many seekers of ancestral wisdom find themselves at this pivotal crossroads, drawn by an irresistible longing for something deeper, something truly rooted in the earth and the unseen currents that shape our lives. They sense the profound magic of the Appalachian mountains, yet struggle to bridge the gap between simple technique and the inherent, living force that gives old ways their undeniable potency. It's a quiet ache, a spiritual hunger for a connection that transcends mere ritual, reaching into the very heart of belief itself. If you've felt this, know that you are not alone in your quest for authentic spiritual engagement.

Perhaps you've explored countless paths, leafing through books that promise a glimpse into the arcane, only to find them offering superficial instructions without the true spiritual context that breathes life into folk magic. You might've diligently followed recipes for tinctures and charms, yet a part of you knew that the ingredients alone were not enough, that a crucial element—a secret ingredient, if you will—remained just out of reach. This longing stems from an innate understanding that true magic is more than just mechanics; it's a living testament to faith, a profound dialogue between the practitioner, the land, and the myriad spirits that inhabit the folds of existence. You crave the kind of wisdom that transforms simple acts into sacred communion, the sort of power that flows not just from what you do, but from what you believe in your very bones.

Imagine a world where your hands, once hesitant over herbs, now move with the instinctive wisdom of generations, your spirit attuned to the very breath of the mountains as if their ancient stories were inscribed upon your soul. Picture yourself not merely performing a spell, but engaging in a profound act of faith, each movement, each whispered word, imbued with an unwavering belief that draws forth genuine healing, potent protection, and an undeniable connection to your ancestors. This is not a fanciful dream but a tangible reality, a way of being that transforms everyday life into a tapestry woven with threads of deep magic and spiritual intentionality. You will learn to walk the path of the mountain witches, not as an imitator, but as a true practitioner, anchored in the living, breathing essence of Appalachian folk magic.

Within these pages, you will discover that the profound essence of Appalachian folk magic lies not just in its whispered incantations or time-honored remedies, but in its very core: an unwavering, faith-infused power that is often overlooked in its study. You stand on the precipice of a transformative journey, one that will take you beyond mere surface practices and into the rich, spiritual tapestry of traditions where belief acts as the true conduit for all magic. Through this unique lens, you will unlock an understanding that shifts your perspective from seeing magic as a collection of acts to experiencing it as a living, breathing faith, potent with ancestral resonance and a deep connection to the natural world. This book promises to guide you to a place where your magic becomes an authentic expression of your deepest spiritual convictions, where every practice resonates with the genuine power born of true belief.

My own journey into these ancient currents began not with a book, but with the earth itself, with the whispering pines and the silent wisdom of stones older than memory. For countless years, I have walked the winding paths of Appalachia, a devoted practitioner and keeper of the old ways, communing with the spirits that linger in the mists and deciphering the subtle language of the wild. My expertise isn't born from fleeting trends or academic study alone, but from a lived, almost primal understanding that magic is fundamentally a living faith, infused with the very essence of profound belief. I've witnessed firsthand how deep spiritual conviction can mend what is broken, protect what is sacred, and bridge the veil between worlds, understanding that true power emerges from the heart, not just the hand.

This isn't simply a collection of spells; it is an invitation into a worldview, a spiritual roadmap unveiled through the subtle authority of one who has truly lived the mountain lore. You will find that I speak with a measured voice, rich with symbolic imagery, guiding you through hidden knowledge with the contemplative wisdom of an elder who has seen the cycles turn and the traditions endure. I am a conduit for generations of arcane wisdom, entrusted with preserving and sharing this sacred heritage, and it is with this deep reverence that I offer you insights that will resonate with your own spiritual hunger, making the arcane accessible yet deeply respected.

Within these pages, you will discover the profound truth that magic is not merely a collection of techniques, but a living, breathing testament to unwavering belief. This foundational understanding, the first secret, reveals how your deepest convictions transform simple actions into potent spiritual acts, creating a direct conduit to the divine forces that govern our world. You will learn how to cultivate your personal faith, recognizing that the power you seek resides not just outside you, but deep within your own spirit, waiting to be awakened.

We will then embark upon the second secret: communing with ancestral and land spirits. Here, you will be guided through ancient pathways of spirit communication, learning practical techniques for meditative listening, crafting personalized ancestral altars, and making sacred offerings that foster profound connections. This communion will not only empower your practice but will also ground you in a deeper understanding of your personal and spiritual identity, allowing you to draw upon a lineage of wisdom and support.

The third secret will immerse you in the sacred practice of wildcrafting, teaching you to approach nature with reverence, seeing every plant and natural element as possessing a spiritual essence. You will learn the art of conscious gathering, asking permission, and expressing gratitude, transforming the act of collecting plant medicine into a sacred ritual that deepens your bond with the earth and enhances the potency of your magical creations for healing and protection. This is not merely about finding herbs, but about fostering a symbiotic relationship with the land itself.

Next, we will unveil the fourth secret: building powerful protection through layered charms and spiritual fortification. You will explore the ancient origins of protective magic in Appalachia, understanding the symbolic meanings and spiritual purposes behind traditional tools and materials. Through detailed instruction, you will learn to craft and empower layered charms, infusing them with focused intent and ancestral blessings, creating an impenetrable shield for yourself, your loved ones, and your home, built on a foundation of profound spiritual fortitude.

The fifth secret reveals the true essence of folk healing remedies, blending ancient plant wisdom with powerful spiritual intention. Here, you will delve into the spiritual properties of healing plants, understanding their unique vibrational energies and how they interact with the human body and spirit. This section moves beyond simple recipes, teaching you to infuse your remedies with focused intent and unwavering faith, transforming them into acts of profound spiritual care and restoration that honor both the physical and unseen aspects of wellbeing.

Finally, we will explore the sixth secret: establishing a rooted personal practice aligned with mountain wisdom. You will learn the art of creating sacred spaces through altar work, choosing and arranging objects that reflect your deepest beliefs and ancestral connections. This section will guide you in honoring the cycles of the seasons, blending Appalachian and Christian traditions into meaningful celebrations, and weaving daily prayer and ritual into the fabric of your life, ensuring your practice is both authentic and deeply personal.

This is more than a guide; it is an invitation to remember, to reconnect, and to reclaim the powerful, faith-infused magic that lies dormant within you, waiting to be awakened by the whispers of the mountains. This journey will offer you not just spells, but a way of life—one that grounds you, empowers you, and reconnects you to the land, the spirits, and the stories that have shaped generations. The profound secrets held within these pages are ready to transform your understanding and practice, weaving the ancient wisdom of Appalachia into the fabric of your modern existence, just as the roots of an old oak intertwine deeply with the earth beneath.

The mountain calls, ancient and resonant, inviting you to remember what your spirit already knows. As we begin, we shall first delve into the very roots of this profound spiritual landscape, exploring the depths of its mysteries and the heights of its wisdom. This journey is not just about learning; it is about becoming, about embodying the magic that has been passed down through the ages, and about finding your place within this timeless tradition. With each step, you will find yourself more deeply connected to the earth, to the spirits, and to the magic that flows through all things. Let us embark on this path together, with open hearts and minds, ready to embrace the mysteries that await.

CHAPTER 1

The Mountain Roots: Understanding Appalachian Folk Magic's Spiritual Foundation

Historical Origins and Cultural Fusion

Celtic Influences and Traditions

When Scottish and Irish immigrants crossed the Atlantic in the 1700s, they carried more than wool blankets and iron pots in their weathered hands. Tucked into memory and woven through bloodline, they brought a complete cosmology of spirits inhabiting every oak tree, every mountain spring, every crossroads where decisions were made and fates were sealed.

These weren't abstract theological concepts discussed in Sunday services. The settlers who ventured into the Appalachian hollows lived daily alongside the *Good Folk*—those elusive spirits who rewarded respect and punished carelessness with equal measure. A farmer knew to leave cream on the doorstep not from charming superstition but from practical necessity, the same way he knew to rotate crops. The boundary between physical and spiritual wasn't a philosophical question but a permeable membrane, crossed routinely through ritual observance and careful attention. Their world pulsed with unseen intelligence, demanding acknowledgment at every turn.

Their herbal knowledge ran deeper than simple remedy lists.

Celtic tradition understood plants as living beings with consciousness, will, and spiritual purpose beyond their chemical compounds. Foxglove wasn't merely digitalis for the heart; it belonged to the fairy realm, dangerous and powerful, requiring permission before harvest. Rowan berries protected against malevolent magic because the tree itself held ancient protective intelligence. This animate understanding of the plant world transferred directly into Appalachian practice, where wildcrafting became a spiritual negotiation rather than mere foraging.

The seasonal wheel turned with sacred precision in Celtic lands, marking moments when the veil thinned and spiritual power intensified. Samhain, Beltane, the solstices—these weren't holidays but cosmic shifts affecting every aspect of magical work and daily survival. When these settlers encountered Appalachian landscapes that mirrored their ancestral mountains, they recognized the land's spiritual architecture immediately. The mist-shrouded peaks, the hidden coves, the mysterious rock formations—all spoke in a familiar language of sacred geography.

What emerged wasn't simple transplantation but something stranger and more potent. The Celtic framework encountered Indigenous wisdom, African spiritual technologies, and the raw power of virgin wilderness itself. In those mountain hollows, separated from old country orthodoxies, these traditions began their slow, deliberate marriage—each contributing essential elements to what would become Appalachian folk magic's unique spiritual foundation.

Indigenous Wisdom and Practices

Long before European ships appeared on distant horizons, the Cherokee and other Indigenous peoples understood the Appalachian mountains as animate spiritual territory. Every ridge, every creek, every stone outcropping possessed consciousness and voice. This wasn't metaphor or poetic license—it was observable reality, verified through generations of careful attention and reciprocal relationship.

The land spoke, and those who listened learned its language.

Indigenous spiritual practice operated on principles of balance and exchange rather than dominion. Harvesting ginseng, for instance, required offering tobacco and speaking directly to the plant's spirit, explaining your need, requesting permission. You never took the first plant you encountered, nor the last, and scattered seeds as payment for what you received (Wetmore, 2021). This wasn't conservation biology dressed in spiritual language; it was recognition that plants possessed agency and memory, that they could withdraw their medicine from those who approached with disrespect or greed.

Water held particular sacred power—springs emerging from deep earth carried messages from the underworld, while flowing streams could wash away spiritual contamination. Certain rock formations served as portals where human and spirit realms intersected, places requiring careful protocol when approached. The Indigenous understanding recognized *thin places* in the landscape where spiritual work intensified naturally, where prayers reached their destinations with greater clarity.

When European settlers arrived with their Celtic cosmology of fairy mounds and sacred wells, they encountered parallel wisdom already embedded in the terrain. Indigenous herbalism, spiritual geography, and animistic worldview didn't conflict with Celtic magical understanding—they reinforced and deepened it. The Cherokee concept of balance, the understanding that every action in the spiritual realm demanded reciprocal exchange, merged seamlessly with Celtic traditions of offering and gratitude. What emerged was not replacement but sacred amplification—two ancient streams of wisdom flowing together, each making the other more potent.

Christianity's Role in Syncretism

Into this convergence of Celtic and Indigenous wisdom walked Christianity, carrying its own potent symbols, stories, and spiritual technologies. But Appalachian folk magic didn't simply adopt Christian elements—it wove them into existing practice with a seamlessness that suggests deeper compatibility than most scholars acknowledge.

The Bible became a talisman itself, placed under pillows to ward off nightmares or opened at random for divination, a practice sometimes referred to as bibliomancy. Psalms transformed into incantations, their rhythmic verses spoken over wounds to stop bleeding or whispered into water for protection baths. For instance, Psalm 23 didn't merely offer comfort—it established spiritual territory, claiming divine protection in language that mirrored Indigenous boundary-setting and Celtic ward-building. (Smith, 2015)

Mountain practitioners recognized no contradiction between Christian prayer and working with plant spirits, between invoking Jesus and reading signs in nature. Both acknowledged an *enchanted cosmos* where spiritual forces responded to human faith and intention.

Biblical symbolism merged with older practices in ways that intensified rather than diluted magical efficacy. The sign of the cross, drawn over doorways or traced in salt, functioned identically to protective sigils from pre-Christian traditions—creating spiritual barriers against malevolent forces. Holy water paralleled the sacred spring water already central to Indigenous practice, used for purification and blessing. The Trinity echoed the three-fold nature of Celtic cosmology, another recognition that power operates in patterns and sacred numbers.

What outsiders sometimes dismiss as "Christian veneer over pagan practice" misunderstands the actual mechanics. Mountain folk weren't disguising their magic in acceptable religious language—they were recognizing genuine spiritual continuity between systems. The Christian God who spoke through burning bushes and parted waters fit naturally into a worldview already acknowledging divine presence in landscape and element. Angels weren't so different from helping spirits; saints became intermediaries much like ancestral guides.

This synthesis created something resilient and adaptive.

When a granny woman spoke healing words over a burn, she might invoke both Cherokee plant wisdom and Christian scripture in the same breath, layering spiritual technologies without hesitation or apology. For instance, some traditional healers might combine the use of specific herbs like bloodroot with prayers from the Bible, demonstrating the seamless integration of these practices in their healing rituals. Faith wasn't divided between traditions—it flowed through all of them, activating their combined power.

The Evolution of a Unique Practice

When travelers moved deeper into Appalachian isolation during the eighteenth and nineteenth centuries, something unexpected happened. The distinct threads—Celtic charm work, Indigenous plant knowledge, Christian prayer—didn't remain separate practices held by different communities. They fused into a single coherent system that mountain people understood as simply "the way things are done."

This matters because isolation preserved what mainstream culture was losing.

While urban centers industrialized and academic medicine displaced folk healing, mountain communities maintained unbroken lineages of practice. Research indicates that traditional healing practices have persisted in Appalachian communities, often passed down through families as living knowledge rather than mere historical curiosity, even as mainstream culture industrialized. The consequences of this preservation extend beyond nostalgia. Mountain magic retained something essential that modern spiritual seekers desperately lack: *embodied faith* that doesn't separate sacred from mundane, prayer from practical action, belief from physical result.

When a practitioner "talks fire" out of a burn or uses red yarn to cure thrush, they're not performing symbolic gestures—they're activating a worldview where words, materials, and faith create tangible change.

This integrated tradition survived precisely because it worked. Families dependent on these practices for healthcare, protection, and community cohesion didn't preserve them out of sentimentality. They continued because results validated belief, and belief strengthened results, creating a self-reinforcing cycle that lasted generations. The emergence of distinct Appalachian folk magic represents more than cultural fusion. It demonstrates how spiritual systems adapt and strengthen through synthesis rather than purity.

What mountain practitioners created—often without formal instruction or written records—was a complete spiritual technology that carried forward the most effective elements from each tradition while remaining flexible enough to absorb new influences without losing coherence.

* * *

SPIRITUAL SYNCRETISM AND THE BIRTH OF A UNIQUE PRACTICE

Cultural Interweaving in Appalachia

Syncretism isn't born from careful planning or theological debate. It emerges when spiritual systems meet and recognize truth in each other, borrowing and blending until something entirely new takes root.

In the isolated hollows of Appalachia, this happened without fanfare or formal declaration. A Scottish woman planted by the moon's phases—Celtic agricultural wisdom passed through her grandmother's hands—while reciting Psalm 121 for protection, the biblical "hills" becoming her literal mountain guardians. She saw no contradiction. Her Cherokee neighbor understood perfectly: both cultures knew that power flows through multiple channels at once, that the sacred world speaks in more than one tongue. (Mc Cauley, 2007)

Watch how a healing ritual evolved in these mountains.

Yarrow, treasured by Celtic healers for wounds and divination, grew wild where Cherokee practitioners already used it to stop bleeding and commune with plant spirits. When a mountain granny gathered this herb, she left tobacco as offering—Indigenous reciprocity—while invoking the Trinity and making the sign of the cross (Hamel & Chiltoskey, 1975). (Hatfield, 2004). The plant responded to all three gestures because the faith behind them was unified, not fragmented. Each layer of belief reinforced the others.

This wasn't casual mixing. This wasn't spiritual confusion borrowing what seemed exotic.

Each element strengthened the whole through what we might call spiritual layering: belief systems stacked like geological strata, each contributing distinct properties. The Christian framework provided moral structure and divine authority. Celtic traditions supplied nature-spirit relationships and awareness of liminal times. Indigenous wisdom offered protocols of reciprocal exchange and deep ecological knowledge. Together, they created practices more resilient than any single tradition could produce alone.

Mountain people didn't theorize about cultural synthesis. They recognized effective practice when they saw it, incorporating what worked while discarding what didn't. Geographic isolation allowed this experimental blending to continue for generations, protected from outside judgment, until the resulting tradition felt seamless—not borrowed fragments, but one coherent spiritual language spoken fluently by those who'd never known any other.

The Role of Faith Traditions

Magic doesn't arise from a vacuum. It grows from the soil of belief, watered by the prayers of those who came before. In the Appalachian mountains, magic emerged from a remarkable convergence of faiths—each tradition bringing its own understanding of the sacred, its own way of speaking to the divine. Christianity arrived with its psalms and holy scriptures, carrying the weight of biblical authority and the comfort of familiar prayers. Indigenous spirituality offered a profound communion with the land itself, teaching that every stone and stream held its own spirit, its own wisdom. When these traditions met in the hollers and on the ridges, they didn't clash. They conversed.

This conversation created something extraordinary. The granny woman who whispered the Lord's Prayer over a poultice knew she was calling on power that transcended any single tradition. Her faith drew from the Bible, yes, but also from the knowing that the earth itself was sacred, that the plants she gathered held spirits willing to aid in healing. She understood that faith was not about choosing one path over another, but about recognizing the divine thread running through all of them. This understanding became the heartbeat of Appalachian magic.

The power in mountain magic flows directly from this multiplicity of belief. When a practitioner lights a candle and speaks an incantation, they aren't simply performing a technique. They're engaging in an act of profound spiritual trust—trust in Christian intercession, trust in ancestral wisdom, trust in the responsive consciousness of nature. Without this layered faith, the magic becomes hollow gesture rather than living practice. The spells work because the practitioner believes they will, and that belief is rooted in generations of validated experience across multiple spiritual frameworks.

Understanding this syncretism means recognizing that Appalachian folk magic was never meant to be pure or singular. Its strength lies precisely in its ability to honor multiple truths simultaneously, to hold

Christianity and earth-reverence in the same hand without contradiction. This is the foundation upon which all mountain magic stands.

Synthesis into Appalachian Magic

Step into this practice by recognizing syncretism isn't something to analyze—it's something to embody. When you begin working Appalachian folk magic, you're not assembling disparate pieces. You're allowing different spiritual currents to flow through your practice until they become indistinguishable from one another.

Start with a simple healing charm. Combine a biblical verse, an offering to the plant spirit, and a physical action rooted in ancestral memory. For a burn, you might whisper Ezekiel's vision of cooling waters while applying fresh plantain leaf, then blow three times across the wound—a gesture older than Christianity itself. These aren't compartmentalized; the verse isn't Christian while the breath is pagan. They function as a single gesture of integrated power.

This is how the mountain practice was truly born.

The old practitioners didn't debate which tradition owned which element. They lived where Celtic memory of protective charms met Cherokee understanding of plant spirits, where Christian prayers for healing intertwined with African practices of spiritual fortification. The magic emerged not from separation but from *synthesis*—each element amplifying the others until something wholly new yet anciently familiar took root in these mountains. Faith became the binding force, the common language spoken by all these traditions, transforming varied practices into a unified whole that carried the power of collective belief.

You'll find this synthesis most powerfully in protection work. A charm bag might contain salt blessed with the Twenty-Third Psalm, roots gathered with gratitude to the land spirits, and a horseshoe nail invoking iron's ancient 守護 power. Each element strengthens the whole, creating layered fortification that draws from multiple wells of spiritual wisdom.

The unique spiritual landscape of these mountains demanded such unity. Isolation and necessity forged practices that worked, regardless of their origin, into a cohesive system that served the people's needs for healing, protection, and connection to the divine.

* * *

The Role of Faith in Mountain Magic

Faith as a Magical Catalyst

Speak a declaration aloud, alone in your space: "I believe this works." Say it three times—once for body, once for mind, once for spirit. Notice what rises in response: that quiet voice of skepticism, the flicker of doubt. Faith isn't the absence of uncertainty; it's the decision to act despite it. Mountain practitioners never waited for proof before beginning their work. They proceeded as though the magic was already alive, and through that very action, their belief deepened into knowing.

Fill a mason jar with spring water. Hold it between your palms and speak your intention directly into the glass—protection, healing, clarity, whatever truth you carry. Don't rush through this like a formula. Feel the water receiving your words, sense it becoming something more than it was moments before. This is *faith made tangible*, belief transferred through focused attention. The old practitioners understood that objects hold what we pour into them, but only when we genuinely trust the exchange happening between our hands.

Each morning, before your feet touch the floor, thank the spirits of your dwelling place. Name them if you know them; if not, address them simply as honored guests sharing your hearth. This practice builds relationship with forces your ancestors understood intimately—the way Slavic traditions honored the *Domovoi*, those benevolent house spirits who received offerings of milk or bread in exchange for protection and prosperity.

Choose one small practice and commit to it for thirty days without measuring outcomes. Light a candle each evening. Speak your protection prayer using whatever words feel true in your mouth. Same gesture, same hour, same intention. Consistency builds spiritual momentum more powerfully than any grand ritual performed once under perfect conditions. The repetition itself becomes belief—muscle memory for the soul.

When doubt surfaces, don't battle it. Acknowledge its presence, then proceed anyway.

The doing strengthens faith more than any internal argument ever could.

Interweaving Faith and Tradition

The Celtic knot patterns inked onto old cabin beams tell the same story as the corn dollies hidden in Appalachian attics: protection through symbols, faith channeled through craft. When Scottish and Irish settlers carried their reverence for standing stones and fairy mounds into the Appalachian hollows, they found Cherokee people who already spoke to the spirits dwelling in mountain laurel and river stones. These weren't opposing worldviews colliding—they were kindred understandings recognizing each other.

The land itself demanded syncretism. You couldn't farm these steep slopes without asking permission from what dwelt there. You couldn't heal fever without both the plant knowledge passed down through grandmothers and the prayers learned in rough-hewn churches. The Bible brought comfort, yes, but so did the old ways of reading signs in bird flight and moon phases. Settlers who insisted on spiritual purity—Celtic only, or Christian only—found their practices hollow, ineffective. The mountains taught a different lesson.

African traditions arrived through the most brutal channels, yet their spiritual technologies proved essential to mountain magic's evolution. Root work, crossroads rituals, the understanding that spirits hunger for specific offerings—these werenings strengthened what was already growing in the hollers. Faith wasn't a single thread but a braid, each strand lending strength to the whole.

This intertwining wasn't theological compromise. It was recognition that the divine speaks through multiple voices simultaneously, and wisdom lies in listening to all of them. The granny woman who could quote Psalms while mixing Cherokee poultices and leaving Celtic knot charms at property corners wasn't confused about her faith—she understood it more completely than those who insisted on singular sources.

Practicing Faith-Driven Magic

Faith isn't something you stumble upon in the woods or find tucked into an old grimoire. It's cultivated, tended like a garden plot on the side of a mountain, requiring your attention, your devotion, and your willingness to show up even when the ground feels hard beneath your feet.

The first step in weaving faith into your practice is recognizing that belief requires daily nourishment. This doesn't mean grand gestures or elaborate ceremonies—though those have their place. It means small, consistent acts of spiritual attention. Light a candle each morning with a prayer of gratitude. Speak aloud your intentions before gathering herbs. Acknowledge the spirits of the land when you walk outside. These seemingly simple practices create a foundation of faith that strengthens over time, building the spiritual muscle memory that transforms ordinary action into sacred work.

Create a personal altar that reflects your spiritual convictions. This sacred space becomes an anchor point for your faith, a physical manifestation of your commitment to the unseen world. Place upon it items that speak to your heart: perhaps a worn Bible that belonged to your grandmother, stones gathered from a mountain stream, dried herbs hanging in bundles, or photographs of ancestors whose wisdom you seek. Tend this altar regularly, not out of obligation but as an act of devotion. Let it evolve as your practice deepens.

Prayer is the language through which faith speaks. In Appalachian tradition, prayer isn't constrained by formality—it's conversation with the divine, whether that's the Christian God, the spirits of the land, or the ancestors who walked these hills before you. Develop a rhythm of prayer that feels authentic to your own spiritual understanding. Pray when you wake, when you work your magic, when you gather plants, when darkness falls. Let your prayers be honest, raw, vulnerable. Faith grows in the soil of genuine communion.

Finally, trust the process of transformation. Faith isn't static; it deepens and shifts as you walk this path. Allow yourself to question, to wrestle with doubt, to seek understanding. The mountain traditions honor this kind of spiritual work, recognizing that *authentic faith is forged through lived experience*, not handed down as doctrine. Your belief becomes powerful precisely because it's yours—earned through practice, nurtured through devotion, and strengthened through the sacred work of showing up, day after day, to tend the fire of your spiritual conviction.

CHAPTER 2

Secret 1: The Power Of Unwavering Belief In Appalachian Practice

The Essence of Belief: Understanding Faith in Magic

F*aith as the Core Element*

A woman in a Kentucky holler once told me she couldn't boil an egg without whispering a blessing over the water first. Not because someone taught her to, but because the act felt *incomplete* otherwise—hollow, unfinished, stripped of meaning. She wasn't performing a ritual. She was acknowledging presence.

That impulse, that bone-deep recognition that words and intention carry weight, is where Appalachian folk magic lives. Not in elaborate ceremonies or ancient grimoires, but in the quiet certainty that speaking to water changes it. That marking a doorway with a cross doesn't just symbolize protection—it *creates* it.

Faith in this tradition isn't abstract theology or Sunday-morning devotion divorced from daily life. It's the active, working conviction that reality responds to human intention when that intention aligns with spiritual truth. A charm bag stuffed with asafoetida and red thread doesn't repel harm because the ingredients possess inherent magical properties (Mythology & Folklore, 2023). (Chireau, 2003). It works because the practitioner believes it works, and that belief opens a channel through which spiritual power flows into material form.

Without this conviction, you're left with theater.

You can memorize every psalm used for protection, gather yarrow at precisely the right moon phase, and arrange your altar with perfect symmetry, but if you're conducting experiments rather than practicing faith, the gestures remain empty. The water stays just water. The cloth stays just cloth. Mountain practitioners understood something most modern seekers struggle with: belief isn't the result of magical success—it's the prerequisite. You don't test whether speaking to your garden makes plants grow better. You speak to your garden because you know plants listen, and that knowing precedes evidence. The results come later, confirming what faith already established. (Yronwode, 2002) (Keville, 2016)

This creates a paradox for newcomers. How do you believe before you have reason to?

How do you cultivate genuine conviction rather than hopeful pretending?

Historical Roots of Belief

Most folk practices don't emerge from single sources. They're born in the friction between worlds, where different peoples meet and their spiritual technologies rub against each other long enough to spark something new.

Appalachian folk magic crystallized in precisely this kind of collision. When Scottish and Irish settlers arrived in these mountains during the 1700s, they carried charm traditions already centuries old—verbal formulas for stopping blood, prayers spoken backward to break curses, the conviction that certain words held power independent of their speakers. They understood *briathra*, the Celtic concept of blessing speech, and they knew that utterances could bind or release spiritual forces.

They didn't arrive in empty territory.

Cherokee and other Indigenous peoples already understood these mountains as animate landscape, where every spring held consciousness and plants required respectful address before harvesting. Their healing practices involved not just botanical knowledge but spiritual negotiation —asking permission, offering tobacco, acknowledging the intelligence residing in root and leaf (Mooney, 1900). When European settlers observed these practices, they recognized something familiar. Not identical, but structurally similar to their own worldview where hawthorn trees guarded thresholds and certain stones carried protective virtue. (Mooney, 1900)

What happened next wasn't appropriation or replacement. It was mutual reinforcement. Both traditions already operated from the same foundational premise: that belief activates power, that speaking with intention alters reality, that the material and spiritual interpenetrate constantly. When a Scottish woman watched a Cherokee healer address tobacco before using it medicinally, she wasn't learning something foreign—she was seeing her own practice of blessing herbs reflected back in different cultural language (Cavender, 2003). When Indigenous peoples heard European charm words, they recognized incantation, just spoken with different syllables. (Cavender, 2003)

Christianity entered this already-blending current not as interruption but as another compatible stream. Psalms became verbal charms because they *were* verbal charms—potent words believed to carry divine force.

Geographic isolation allowed this synthesis to deepen across generations without external correction or standardization. Families practiced what worked, and what worked was increasingly hybrid—Cherokee plant knowledge spoken over with Irish blessings, biblical verses folded into Indigenous understandings of reciprocal exchange with the land. Belief intensified through results, creating self-sustaining cycles where faith generated outcomes that validated faith. Each generation inherited not just techniques but the profound conviction that made those techniques effective, until faith itself became the tradition's most powerful inheritance.

Cultivating Personal Faith

When you first come to this work, you might carry a particular burden: the notion that magic demands perfection. That words must be spoken exactly right, ingredients measured to the grain, timing precise to the second. This anxiety reveals a deeper misunderstanding about where the true power lives.

Faith doesn't require perfection. It requires honesty.

The old mountain practitioners understood this in their bones. When a grandmother whispered words over a bleeding wound, she didn't pause to wonder if her phrasing matched some distant authority. She spoke with *conviction*, and that conviction became the medicine itself (Hand, 1980). Her certainty that the words would work made them work —not through wishful thinking, but because unwavering belief creates the spiritual conditions where power flows freely. The words were merely the channel; her faith was the current running through it. (Hand, 1980)

This matters because doubt is what stops most people before they even begin. We've grown up questioning everything, trained to demand proof before we'll believe anything. That skepticism serves us well in some parts of life. In folk magic, though, it acts like static on a radio signal, scrambling the very frequency that carries the work.

You cannot craft a protection charm while simultaneously doubting whether protection charms function. That split in your mind undermines the focused intention the work requires. Magic needs unified belief—not blind faith, but the willingness to set internal argument aside long enough to speak your intention into being without hedging, without building in excuses, without the comfort of "well, nothing will probably happen anyway."

The proof comes through doing, not through studies or charts. Families kept these practices alive across generations because they worked—wounds stopped bleeding, fevers broke, troubled relationships found peace (Wigginton, 1972). When results follow practice over and over, belief grows naturally. As belief deepens, the work grows stronger. The cycle feeds itself, but only if you step fully into it rather than watching from the outside.

So how do you build genuine faith when you've been taught to question everything?

Through deliberate practice, the same way you'd strengthen any other capacity. Faith isn't something you either have or don't—it's something you develop through use. Each time you speak a blessing over water and drink it as though it carries exactly what you named, you're exercising belief. Each time you mark your doorway for protection and walk through trusting that boundary holds, you're building the internal certainty that makes your next working more potent.

* * *

Intention as a Magical Tool: Directing Spiritual Energy

Defining Magical Intention

Magical intention is the conscious, focused will that transforms ordinary action into spiritual work. When a mountain woman stirs salt into water for cleansing, the circular motion of her hand is not what makes it medicine—her deliberate direction of purpose through that gesture is what opens the channel for spiritual power to flow. Without this focused will, she's simply dissolving sodium chloride.

Intention operates as the bridge between thought and manifestation. You cannot accidentally perform effective folk magic any more than you can accidentally speak fluent Cherokee. The words might be correct, the herbs properly gathered, the moon phase favorable, but if your mind wanders while you work—if you're mentally rehearsing tomorrow's errands while tying a protection cord—you're enacting theater, not conjure.

This differs fundamentally from wishful thinking or vague hope.

When an Appalachian practitioner sets intention, she specifies exactly what spiritual energy she's directing and toward what purpose. "I want things to get better" carries no targeting information, no vector for power to follow. "I direct protection around this threshold against all harm intended for those who dwell here" creates a precise channel. The universe responds to clarity the way water responds to a carved irrigation ditch—it flows where directed, not where you generally hope it might go.

The old-timers understood this implicitly. A great-grandfather performing *Braucherei*, a Pennsylvania Dutch folk healing practice, didn't hope words might help with burns or wish for relief (Kriebel,

2007). Instead, practitioners would often perform *Pustere*, or "blowing the fire out" of a burn, by directing healing force through specific verbal formulas and their breath, with their entire being aligned behind the work (Hoplon Designs, 2026). This practice, often involving the "Rule of Three"—three breaths, three spoken charms, or rituals over three days —binds the intention directly to the physical realm (Hoplon Designs, 2026; Reddit, 2022). His attention never wavered from the burn to the blessing and back again. That unwavering focus, sustained throughout the working, acted as the mechanism through which spiritual energy entered physical reality.

Intention requires presence. You cannot text while crafting a charm bag and expect potency. The work demands your complete attention in that moment, your will gathered and aimed like lamplight through a lens, concentrating diffuse possibility into focused beam.

Crafting Purposeful Intentions

Folk traditions throughout the mountains show practitioners engaging in dedicated preparation before any healing or protective working. An experienced practitioner addressing a persistent ailment doesn't rush into ritual. She cultivates focused intention through specific preparatory steps that transform vague hope into precise spiritual force.

This preparation might involve quiet contemplation for several days. Each morning, the practitioner spends time with a symbolic object, speaking her intention aloud—perhaps to "draw imbalance from the flesh and restore health." This repetition, with consistent words and unwavering focus, builds power. On the day of the working, she performs the final steps while maintaining the singular focus she's been cultivating since she began. What matters isn't whether skeptics credit placebo or spontaneous recovery.

What matters is the methodical construction of focused will before she ever touched the affected individual.

She didn't improvise. She didn't hope vaguely for improvement while her mind wandered to grocery lists. She built her intention deliberately, word by word, day by day, until the channel between thought and physical outcome became clear enough for power to flow through. This three-day preparation period appears throughout Appalachian practice because *sustained focus* strengthens intention beyond what single-moment willpower can achieve. A practitioner crafting protection doesn't simply decide "I want safety" and proceed immediately to tying red thread. She might spend days sitting with exactly what protection means in this context—protection from what, protection for whom, protection manifesting how. Each time she returns to these questions, her intention clarifies and consolidates like water freezing into ice.

The Foxfire interviews from the 1970s documented similar patterns. Elderly practitioners described the methodical process of working intentions as akin to tending coals—you don't build a fire by scattered, intermittent attention; you feed it consistently, tend it deliberately, and maintain focus until the heat becomes self-sustaining.

This cultivation period serves another purpose: it reveals uncertainty. If you cannot maintain consistent intention across three days, you've discovered where doubt still scrambles your signal, where your will needs strengthening before the actual working begins.

Rituals for Intention Setting

Sustained intention requires actual structure. Morning devotion provides this—five minutes before the day fragments your attention into competing demands. Begin with a candle and a glass of water on a stable surface. Light the candle while speaking your intention aloud, using identical words each morning. "I call forth protection for this household" or "I draw health into my body" or whatever specific outcome you're building toward. Speak it three times, then drink the water.

This becomes non-negotiable routine, practiced whether you feel inspired or distracted or skeptical. The repetition itself builds power, independent of your mood.

Traditional practitioners often kept a small notebook recording intentions and outcomes. Not elaborate journaling—just date, stated intention, and later notation of results. This practice serves dual purposes: it trains you to speak intentions with precision rather than vague yearning, and it creates accountability. Writing "protection from financial loss" on Monday forces you to recognize when Thursday's intention has drifted to "general abundance" or dissolved into unfocused anxiety. The notebook reveals where your focus fragments before you waste energy on scattered workings.

Evening practice creates closure.

Return to the candle at day's end, restate your intention once, and extinguish the flame with gratitude—not for results you're hoping to manifest, but for the spiritual channel you've spent the day maintaining. This acknowledgment matters because folk magic understands reciprocity as fundamental (Danalis, 2019; Healthmantra, n.d.; Morrison, 2018; Rankin, 2019; Cailleachs Herbarium, 2016). You're working with forces that respond to respect and consistent attention, not demands lobbed sporadically into the void whenever crisis strikes.

When intention-setting fails, the breakdown usually occurs in one of three places. First: the stated intention conflicts with unconscious resistance. Someone speaking protection while believing they deserve punishment creates opposing currents that cancel each other. Second: the intention lacks genuine specificity. "I want things to get better" gives spiritual forces nothing concrete to work with—it's static, not signal. Third, and most common, the practitioner abandons consistent practice after three days without visible results, not recognizing that *building the channel precedes evidence flowing through it (Pavlina, 2006; Healthmantra, n.d.; Danalis, 2025).*. Mountain grandmothers understood what impatient seekers forget: you don't test whether the well works before you finish digging it.

Channeling Energy Through Belief

Belief channels spiritual energy through intention, but only when rooted in disciplined practice. Start with something real: protection for your child, healing from injury, resolution of a pressing financial need. Write it as a single, unqualified sentence: "My daughter travels safely to and from school," not "I hope my daughter might be protected if possible." Precision matters.

Choose one physical object to hold this intention. Traditional practitioners favored threshold items—a stone from the doorstep, water from a boundary creek, a key. The object itself matters less than your consistency with it. Place it where you'll encounter it multiple times daily: kitchen windowsill, bedside table, workspace. Each time you see it during the first week, speak your intention aloud. Not paraphrased. Exact words, repeated.

This will feel absurd.

You'll hear yourself and think you sound foolish or desperate. Speak anyway. By day three, the words should flow without conscious retrieval. By day seven, seeing the object triggers automatic recitation. This is when the working truly begins—not when you decided to try folk magic, but when repetition has carved the intention into your nervous system deeply enough that conscious effort becomes unnecessary. Many traditional practices emphasize that verbal formulas need to reach the level of reflex, becoming deeply ingrained before they register as genuine call rather than passing whim.

After two weeks of daily repetition, reduce frequency to morning and evening only, but add a physical gesture. Touch the object while speaking, or trace a cross over it, or hold it against your heart. The gesture links body to intention, creating what traditional workers understood as a complete circuit—thought shaped into speech, speech anchored in matter, matter held by flesh. Your full being participates, not just your hopeful thinking.

Track small shifts, not miracles. Your daughter mentions a near-miss that didn't happen. The injury's inflammation decreases slightly. An unexpected twenty dollars appears. These aren't coincidences to dismiss or dramatic validations to trumpet—they're the first trickle indicating your channel is opening. Note them without fanfare, then return to consistent practice. Faith deepens through accumulated minor evidence, not lightning-strike conversion. You're building a well, and the water rises slowly from below.

* * *

Cultivating Personal Faith: Connecting with the Divine

Recognizing Divine Presence

Recognizing the divine woven through your daily life requires training your attention, not waiting for revelation. This week, choose one recurring activity you already perform—washing dishes, brewing coffee, walking to check the mail. Before you begin, pause. Place your hand on your chest and speak aloud: "I open my eyes to what's already here." Then proceed with heightened awareness, noticing details you typically ignore.

The divine doesn't arrive in lightning bolts for most practitioners. It appears in the way morning light falls through a particular window, creating a golden path across your floor each dawn. It manifests in the cardinal that returns to your porch rail, the unexpected scent of rosemary when no rosemary grows nearby, the sudden stillness before rain. These aren't coincidences or random occurrences—they're sacred signs, subtle communications from the spiritual realm that surrounds and permeates everything you touch, see, and experience.

When you begin to perceive these patterns, your magical practice transforms.

The herbs you gather become more than ingredients; they're allies you've been introduced to by the land itself. The water you bless carries not just your intention but the *recognition* of its inherent holiness. Your protection charms gain power because you're no longer working alone —you're collaborating with forces that have been reaching toward you all along, waiting for you to notice. Faith deepens not through dramatic conversion but through this patient, daily witnessing of the sacred woven into ordinary moments, until the distinction between mundane and magical dissolves entirely.

Building a Personal Relationship

Most practitioners stumble not from lack of ability but from expecting too much, too fast. You'll light your first candle, speak your first prayer, and wait for unmistakable divine response—a voice, a vision, undeniable proof. When silence follows, doubt creeps in. This is the first obstacle, and it defeats more seekers than any lack of natural talent ever could.

Progress in this work happens in whispers, not shouts. The divine conversation you're building develops like any relationship worth having —through consistent presence, not perfect performance. Your grandmother didn't master cornbread on her first attempt. She burned batches, adjusted proportions, learned her oven's particular temperament through failure and repetition. Spiritual connection follows identical principles.

Start where you actually are, not where you imagine you should be. If formal prayer feels awkward and artificial in your mouth, speak plainly. Tell the divine what troubles you in the same words you'd use with a trusted friend. If sitting still for meditation makes your skin crawl, walk your land instead, letting your feet create the rhythm that opens your attention. Even within established traditions, many forms of contemplative prayer or mindfulness meditation encourage tailoring techniques to an individual's unique temperament and daily life, emphasizing genuine engagement over strict ritual.

Common obstacles have common solutions.

When doubt arrives—and it will—don't fight it or pretend it doesn't exist. Acknowledge it directly: *"I'm uncertain today, but I'm showing up anyway."* Then proceed with your practice exactly as planned. Faith isn't the absence of doubt; it's continuing the work despite doubt's presence. Some mornings your altar devotion will feel hollow, your words will sound like noise, and nothing will shift perceptibly. Do it anyway. The channel you're carving operates beneath conscious awareness, and consistency matters more than emotional certainty.

Track small shifts in a dedicated notebook. Not dramatic visions—notice instead that your sleep improved after three nights of evening prayer. That unexpected help arrived the day after you asked for guidance. That you felt calmer entering a difficult conversation after morning candle work. These minor confirmations accumulate into unshakeable knowing, but only if you record them. Memory deceives; written evidence builds faith that survives dry periods when nothing seems to work and the divine feels distant as stars.

Expressing Faith Through Ritual

Belief without practice remains theoretical. Practice without belief becomes empty repetition. What unites them—what transforms both into genuine spiritual power—is ritual designed from your actual faith, not borrowed wholesale from someone else's understanding.

Personalized ritual creates the container where your unique spiritual relationship can grow. This doesn't mean inventing practices from nothing or disregarding tradition. It means recognizing that the mountain practitioners who came before you also adapted, modified, and created new expressions as their understanding deepened. They didn't follow rigid formulas; they honored the spirit of the work while letting their personal connection to the divine shape the details.

Consider the granny woman who always said the Lord's Prayer backward for protection work, or the one who wove psalms into her herb gathering. These weren't standard practices written in any book—they emerged from individual spiritual conversations with the divine. Your rituals can do the same.

Start with what already resonates in your spiritual life. If you pray daily, that prayer becomes the foundation for ritual work. If you find the divine in morning coffee or evening walks, those moments can transform into sacred practice. The power lies not in exotic gestures but in authentic alignment between your actions and your faith.

Maybe you light a candle each time you work magic, speaking your intention as the flame catches. Maybe you keep a small bowl of water on your altar, changing it with the moon and offering thanks as you pour the old water onto your garden. Maybe you recite a specific biblical verse before gathering plants, or sing a hymn your grandmother taught you.

Whatever form it takes, your ritual should feel like coming home to yourself spiritually—not like performing someone else's choreography. When ritual becomes this personal expression of faith, it stops being something you *do* and becomes something you *are*. That's when the real magic begins.

CHAPTER 3

Secret 2: Communing With Ancestral And Land Spirits For Empowered Practice

---

The Historical Pathways of Spirit Communication

Ancient Appalachian Practices

When the first European settlers moved into the hollows of Appalachia, they brought with them a vocabulary for spirit contact that predated Christian missionaries by centuries. They consulted the dead at crossroads after midnight, left milk for household spirits, and watched for animal messengers that carried warnings from the otherworld. These weren't superstitions grafted awkwardly onto frontier life.

Spirit communication formed the practical infrastructure of survival, as essential as knowing which mushrooms were safe to eat. A grandmother might receive planting instructions from her deceased husband in dreams. A child who saw lights moving through the woods knew to follow or flee based on their color and behavior. The boundary between living and dead remained permeable by necessity—ancestors held knowledge about weather patterns, medicinal plants, and threats the newly arrived couldn't yet recognize.

Cherokee and other Indigenous peoples already living in these mountains operated from similar cosmological assumptions, though their specific practices differed. They understood certain locations as thin places where spirits congregated, performed ceremonies to maintain reciprocal relationships with land guardians, and recognized that disrespecting these protocols invited tangible consequences.

When European and Indigenous communities interacted, they found common ground in their shared conviction that the invisible world demanded attention and negotiation. The resulting practices blended methods with remarkable fluidity. Evidence suggests settlers adopted the Indigenous custom of leaving tobacco as offering, a practice integral to many North American Indigenous spiritual traditions for communication with the spirit world, giving thanks, and seeking guidance. Simultaneously, some Cherokee families incorporated Biblical psalms into protection rituals, blurring the lines between prayer and folk magic (Association of Independent Readers and Rootworkers, n.d.). (River Wind & River Wind, 2018; Association of Independent Readers and Rootworkers, n.d.). Both traditions valued intermediary objects—stones, bones, specially prepared bundles—that anchored spiritual presence in physical form. Both recognized practitioners with natural sensitivity to spirit contact, individuals who seemed born with thinner veils between worlds.

Ceremonial structures emerged organically from this convergence. Spirit communication often occurred at boundary times—dawn, dusk, the turn of seasons—and boundary places where forest met field or streams converged. Practitioners prepared themselves through fasting, prayer, or ritual bathing, creating internal receptivity to match external conditions. The actual contact might involve direct speech, symbolic interpretation of natural signs, or entering trance states that contemporary observers would struggle to distinguish from Indigenous vision quests or Celtic shamanic journeys.

These weren't recreational explorations of mystical states. Families consulted spirits to locate lost livestock, identify thieves, diagnose mysterious illnesses, and receive warnings about impending danger. The effectiveness of these practices reinforced their continuation across generations, creating lineages of spirit workers whose authority derived from demonstrated results rather than institutional credentials.

Cultural Syncretism and Evolution

African spiritual technologies arrived through the bodies of enslaved people, carriers of West African cosmologies that recognized ancestors as active participants in daily life and understood spirit possession as communication rather than pathology. These traditions recognized crossroads as spiritually charged locations, practiced divination through cast objects, and maintained elaborate systems for honoring the dead whose favor or displeasure directly affected the living. The wisdom they carried wasn't written in books but embedded in ritual memory, passed through generations despite deliberate attempts to erase it.

The convergence wasn't simply additive.

When European graveyard dirt traditions, which often involved using grave earth for protection or cursing, met African practices of collecting cemetery soil for specific spiritual purposes, they didn't just coexist—they amplified each other through recognition of shared logic. Both understood that bones held power, that certain locations accumulated spiritual charge, that material objects could house non-physical presences. The resulting Appalachian approach to spirit contact drew from all three streams without requiring practitioners to acknowledge or even recognize the multiple origins, creating something both practical and profoundly reverent.

A mountain practitioner in 1820 might burn sage while reciting the Twenty-Third Psalm and pouring whiskey at a crossroads, each element derived from different cultural sources but functioning as integrated spiritual technology. The sage carried Indigenous associations with purification and spirit contact, drawing on local plant knowledge. The psalm provided Christian framing that made the practice socially acceptable while adding genuine spiritual force through biblical authority. The crossroads offering reflected African cosmological principles about liminal spaces where spiritual commerce occurred.

Cultural syncretism describes this process—the blending of different belief systems into new, functional wholes that exceed their component parts.

Appalachian spirit communication became something genuinely

novel, neither purely Celtic nor Indigenous nor African but authentically synthesized into practices that addressed the specific spiritual and practical needs of mountain communities. This synthesis remained dynamic rather than fixed. As circumstances changed, practices evolved while maintaining core principles. The fundamental conviction that spirits could be contacted, negotiated with, and enlisted for practical purposes survived regardless of which specific methods proved most effective in particular situations or generations. Faith itself became the constant thread weaving through all variations.

Impact on Modern Practices

These historical pathways matter because authentic spiritual connection doesn't emerge from fabricated rituals or superficial borrowing. When contemporary practitioners approach Appalachian folk magic as mere aesthetic—collecting mason jars and vintage handkerchiefs without understanding the belief systems that made those objects spiritually active—they practice theater, not magic. The tradition works because generations of mountain people staked their lives on it, refining techniques through immediate necessity. A failed healing charm meant a child's fever continued. An ineffective protection ritual meant livestock died. The practices that survived did so because they consistently produced results that reinforced belief, creating the very faith that powered subsequent workings.

Modern practitioners inherit this accumulated spiritual momentum.

When you speak to land spirits using adapted Cherokee protocols, you're not appropriating but participating in the same synthesis that mountain families developed through generations of reciprocal relationship with specific territories. The mountain laurel doesn't distinguish between your ancestry and your genuine respect. What matters is whether you approach with the humility that characterized all three contributing traditions—the Celtic understanding that spirits demanded proper protocol, the Indigenous recognition that plants and places possessed agency deserving negotiation, the Christian framework that required petition rather than command.

Contemporary adaptation requires discernment about what elements carry spiritual weight versus cultural decoration. A practitioner today might use a smartphone timer instead of watching candle marks to measure ritual duration, but the underlying principle—that focused attention sustained over specific time periods builds spiritual momentum—remains unchanged. The *technology* shifts while the spiritual logic persists.

Connecting with ancestral spirits through these historical pathways offers something Instagram witchcraft cannot: legitimacy earned through survival. Your great-grandmother who whispered prayers over sick children, who buried coins at property corners, who knew which phase of the moon governed which workings—she practiced this tradition when it cost something to be called a witch, when neighbors might shun or worse. That continuity carries power.

Even practitioners without Appalachian ancestry can access these pathways through the spirits of place themselves.

The mountains remember. The plants still respond. The crossroads retain their charge.

* * *

Practical Techniques for Communing with Spirits

Meditative Spirit Listening

This isn't passive waiting. Setting intention functions as the spiritual equivalent of tuning a radio to the correct frequency. Before attempting contact, you must know exactly what you're listening for: guidance about a specific problem, wisdom from a particular ancestor, messages from the land spirits of your home ground. Vague openness invites confusion. Precision creates clarity.

The physical preparation matters less than consistent execution. Some practitioners sit at their ancestor altar with a single white candle. Others walk the same forest path at dawn for seven consecutive days. The pattern resembles certain Eastern spiritual traditions, where individuals commit to daily exercises—often at fixed times—to cultivate discipline and receptivity. What each approach shares is *deliberate repeti-*

tion. Spirits learn where to find you when you show up reliably, in the same internal state, with the same openness.

Your nervous system requires training too. The first attempts feel like self-delusion, internal dialogue disguised as contact. But sustained practice develops discernment between your own mental chatter and the distinct quality of received information: unexpected images, knowledge you didn't previously possess, physical sensations that carry meaning. The difference becomes unmistakable with time.

Cultivating an open heart means releasing attachment to specific answers. You're not demanding spirits confirm what you already believe but genuinely asking what you need to know. This vulnerability requires faith—the understanding that ancestral and land spirits operate from broader perspective than immediate human desire.

Sometimes the guidance arrives as uncomfortable truth. Sometimes it unfolds over weeks through accumulated small signs. The practice deepens through patient consistency, not dramatic breakthroughs.

Creating Ancestral Altars

An ancestral altar creates physical space for spiritual conversation. Not decoration, not memorial—an active threshold where you meet those who came before.

Start with a surface set apart from daily life. Cover it with clean cloth, preferably in colors that held meaning for your people—white for purity, black for protection, red for life force. Upon this foundation, arrange objects that carried your ancestors' touch. A grandmother's thimble worn smooth by decades of mending. A great-uncle's knife, its blade thin from sharpening. These items don't merely represent the dead; they hold residual energy from years of contact, creating what practitioners call a spiritual signature—the accumulated essence of a life lived.

Photographs anchor the work, but choose carefully. Formal portraits lack vitality. Instead, seek images capturing genuine expression: your grandfather mid-laugh, your aunt's hands kneading bread, a great-grandmother standing in her garden with dirt under her fingernails. These candid moments preserve character, and character is what you're inviting into relationship.

Offerings sustain connection. Leave fresh water daily—it represents life itself, perpetually renewed. Add foods they favored in this world: black coffee for the uncle who rose before dawn, cornbread for the granny who fed everyone who crossed her threshold, whiskey for the ancestor who appreciated its warmth. These aren't bribes but gestures of continued care, proving the relationship remains alive despite the boundary of death.

Light a white candle when you approach the altar. This simple act signals intentional communion, illuminating both physical space and the subtle realm where spirits dwell. Speak aloud—share family news, ask for guidance on troubles weighing heavy, or simply maintain conversation as you would with the living. Your voice carries across the veil.

Placement matters deeply. This sacred work demands privacy, protection from casual interruption or curious hands that don't understand. A bedroom corner, a dedicated room, even a sheltered outdoor space near family graves—choose location based on accessibility and reverence. The altar must be reachable for daily tending yet separate from household traffic.

Maintain it faithfully. Dust signals neglect; wilted flowers and stale water suggest abandonment. Your ancestors respond to consistent attention, to proof that you honor the relationship through regular care.

Offering Rituals and Practices

Offerings aren't decoration. They're spiritual currency, the language through which respect becomes tangible and invitation becomes mutual.

Food offerings carry the most direct power because they address fundamental need. Spirits don't hunger as the living do, but the *gesture* of feeding creates bonds that transcend both realms. Staple foods like cornbread and milk, common in Appalachian households, work well because of their simplicity—these were foods that sustained mountain families through hardship, foods that ancestors actually ate and valued. Leave portions at your altar before dawn, speaking clearly about what relationship you're cultivating. Land spirits favor tobacco, whiskey, or honey left at the base of old trees.., particularly where roots break through earth in gnarled exposure. Ancestral spirits appreciate foods they loved in life: a grandmother's preferred pie, coffee prepared exactly as your grandfather took it, salt pork for those who knew genuine hunger.

The timing of offering matters as much as content. Dawn and dusk —threshold times when day meets night—carry natural openings between worlds. These liminal moments amplify spiritual receptivity, making your gesture more likely to reach its intended recipient.

But offerings can fail spectacularly when motivation sours the exchange. Spirits recognize transactional desperation, the energetic stink of someone who gives only to extract. If you approach with entitled expectation—*I left cornbread, so fix my problem now*—you'll find doors closing rather than opening. The relationship must develop through consistency before asking for intervention. Three months of regular offerings without petition builds more power than a year of desperate bargaining.

Fresh flowers honor without feeding, their beauty and inevitable decay mirroring the cycle of life and death that binds you to ancestors. Wildflowers gathered from land you tend carry more power than expensive grocery store bouquets because they connect to place, to the actual earth your spirits knew or now inhabit. Replace them before they rot—death has already claimed these spirits; don't offer them additional decay.

Some offerings fail because they're historically hollow.

Burning expensive incense your ancestors never encountered, leaving foods from cultures they'd find alien, speaking in formal language they never used—these gestures carry no authentic spiritual weight. Your great-grandmother who spoke mountain dialect and cooked on a wood stove won't respond to Sanskrit chants and exotic fruits. Watch for acceptance signs: candle flames that burn unusually steady, food that disappears faster than natural decay explains, dreams arriving within days of new offerings. Rejection manifests as spoilage, repeatedly extinguished flames, or deepening silence where you hoped for contact.

Nature Immersion and Spirit Walks

Choose your route before you leave the house. Spirit walks require intentionality from the first step—this isn't recreational hiking or exercise dressed up as spiritual practice. Select a place that pulls at you, somewhere you've felt watched or strangely comfortable, where silence feels thick rather than empty. Old logging roads, abandoned homesteads, creek beds twisting through unmanaged forest—these hold more spiritual residue than maintained trails where thousands pass weekly.

Leave your phone behind or silence it completely.

Spirits communicate through subtle shifts in attention, and distraction creates static that drowns their whispers. Before entering the woods, pause at the threshold—the point where maintained ground gives way to wildness. Speak aloud your intention: *"I come to listen. I come to learn. I mean no disrespect to those who dwell here."* Simple words matter more than elaborate invocations. You're announcing yourself, establishing that you understand you're entering inhabited territory requiring permission.

Walk slowly enough to notice. Most people move through nature at a pace designed to reach destinations, but spirit walks have no destination beyond presence itself. When something catches your attention—an unusual stone, a tree growing in a strange pattern, a bird that doesn't flee your approach—stop completely. These aren't random moments. Spirits often communicate through what draws your eye, using the landscape itself as vocabulary. A hawk circling three times overhead, a sudden wind when air has been still, finding a perfect walking stick exactly when your knee starts aching—pay attention to timing and repetition.

Touch things. Press your palm against old-growth bark. Sit on exposed roots. Wade into the creek if it calls you. Physical contact creates energetic exchange that observation alone cannot. The land spirits aren't abstract entities—they're bound to actual matter, and your body touching their domain opens communication channels that thinking about nature never will.

Bring tobacco or cornmeal in your pocket. When you feel particularly drawn to a spot, leave a small offering without ceremony or expectation. This teaches reciprocity through action, building relationship muscle memory that will serve every future working.

Don't force messages or interpret every rustling leaf as profound sign. Real communication often arrives hours or days later—in dreams, through sudden knowing, or as information that surfaces when you're washing dishes. The walk itself plants seeds that germinate on their own schedule.

* * *

The Spiritual Benefits of Ancestral and Land Spirit Connection

Empowerment Through Ancestral Bonds

You already carry the resonance of your ancestors in your very bones, whether you've acknowledged them or not. Their struggles, their survival, their small triumphs against impossible odds—all of it lives in you as potential waiting to be recognized and activated. When you forge an intentional bond with ancestral spirits, you're not reaching into empty air hoping for phantoms. You're tuning yourself to a frequency that's been broadcasting your entire life, strengthening a connection that biology began but conscious devotion completes.

This connection transforms how you understand yourself. You stop being an isolated individual stumbling through decisions alone and become instead the living continuation of a lineage that solved problems, endured hardships, and preserved wisdom specifically so you could exist. When you face uncertainty, ancestral connection offers guidance not as abstract inspiration but as tangible presence—the sudden memory of how your grandmother handled conflict, the inexplicable confidence that arrives when attempting something unfamiliar, the dream that delivers exactly the insight you needed but couldn't consciously access.

Your magical practice gains depth it cannot achieve through solitary effort. Every protection spell becomes anchored in generations of survived threats. Every healing remedy carries the accumulated knowledge of those who worked with the same plants, facing the same ailments, refining what works through lifetimes of careful observation. The roots you establish through ancestral connection don't just support your work—they amplify it, lending power that individual faith alone cannot generate.

Land spirits offer different gifts but equally profound ones. Where ancestors provide lineage and identity, land spirits teach belonging and reciprocity. When you establish relationship with the spirits of place—the genius loci that inhabits the mountain hollow, the creek bed, the ancient oak—you learn to move through the world as participant rather than trespasser. The land begins offering what you need: the specific herb appearing exactly when required, the weather shifting to protect your garden, the sudden knowing of where to walk safely in darkness.

This isn't imagination or wishful projection. It's the natural result of sustained, respectful attention combined with reciprocal exchange. Land spirits respond to presence the way any relationship deepens through consistency—slowly, testing your sincerity, then opening with startling generosity once trust establishes. They guide your wildcrafting so you harvest without harm. They warn you of danger through sensation and instinct. They teach you to read the world's subtle language: what the wind's direction means, what bird behavior signals, what the quality of silence indicates.

Together, ancestral and land spirit connections create what nothing else in Appalachian folk magic can replicate: rooted authenticity. You stop practicing magic as though following instructions from a manual and begin working as someone who belongs to a living tradition, supported by both lineage and landscape. Your faith deepens because it's not abstract belief but daily confirmation—spirits respond, guidance arrives, impossible coincidences accumulate until you cannot dismiss them.

This rootedness protects against the spiritual hollowness that plagues much modern practice. You're not alone, improvising rituals from fragments and hoping for the best. You're embedded in relationship, upheld by forces older and wiser than yourself, practicing magic that carries the weight and power of continuity. The ancestors and land spirits don't just observe your work—they participate in it, lending their strength to yours, transforming solitary effort into collaboration across the boundaries of time and form.

Harmony with the Land's Spirit

Building these connections doesn't happen overnight, and that matters more than you might think. The slow unfolding teaches patience that becomes its own spiritual discipline. You begin with offerings that feel awkward, meditations where nothing seems to happen, walks where the land stays silent. Then one morning you wake knowing your grandmother wants you to visit her grave. Or you find yourself avoiding a trail for no logical reason, only to learn later that a tree fell exactly where you would have walked.

Small confirmations arrive like drops of water—individually unremarkable, cumulatively undeniable.

Trust the slowness. It's not failure or evidence of inadequacy. It's the natural rhythm of relationship-building across the veil, where spirits test sincerity through sustained effort rather than dramatic declarations. What you've learned in this chapter forms the foundation for everything that follows. Ancestral connection roots you in lineage, giving your practice historical weight and inherited power. Land spirit relationship embeds you in place, teaching reciprocity and belonging that transforms how you move through the world.

Together they create the relational matrix that makes Appalachian folk magic something more than technique—they make it a living tradition you participate in rather than merely perform. The practical methods matter: building altars with intention, making offerings with consistency, walking the land with respectful attention, cultivating receptivity through disciplined listening. But the deeper work happens in how these practices reshape your understanding of yourself.

You're no longer an isolated practitioner hoping rituals work through sheer willpower.

You're embedded in relationship with forces that actively support your efforts, guide your decisions, and lend their strength to yours. This changes everything about how magic functions. Your spell for protection carries ancestral memory of survived threats. Your healing work draws on land wisdom about which plants grow where and why. Your divination opens to guidance from sources that see beyond your limited perspective. The magic becomes collaborative rather than solitary, amplified through connection rather than dependent solely on personal power.

Keep tending what you've begun. Refresh that altar water daily even when nothing dramatic happens. Leave those offerings at the old oak's roots even when you're tired and it seems pointless. Speak to your ancestors even when doubt whispers that you're talking to empty air. The relationship deepens through faithful consistency, not through sporadic intensity or desperate bargaining. Watch for the shifts: dreams that carry unusual clarity, coincidences that accumulate past randomness, instincts that prove accurate more often than chance explains.

These aren't proof you can display to skeptics, but they're confirmation enough for the practitioner who experiences them repeatedly.

Your nervous system learns to recognize genuine contact, and faith stops being abstract belief and becomes instead the rational response to accumulated evidence. What comes next builds directly on this foundation. You cannot practice effective protection magic, healing work, or divination without the relational matrix you're establishing now. The spirits you're learning to commune with don't just support your practice—they make certain kinds of work possible that individual effort alone cannot achieve.

So tend these relationships with the same care you'd give any connection that matters, because they do matter. More than you yet realize.

CHAPTER 4

Secret 3: Sacred Wildcrafting And The Conscious Gathering Of Plant Medicine

Understanding the Sacred Bond with Nature

Nature's Spiritual Essence

The old ones knew something most of us have forgotten: every plant breathes with its own spirit. The foxglove at the forest edge, the sassafras root beneath your feet, the wild ginger hiding in the shade—they're not just botanical specimens waiting to be plucked. They're living beings with consciousness, memory, and purpose. When you approach wildcrafting with this understanding, everything changes. You're no longer simply harvesting materials for your remedies and charms. You're entering into relationship with powers far older than any human tradition.

This belief in plant consciousness forms the bedrock of authentic Appalachian wildcrafting. It's the difference between mechanical gathering and sacred communion, between a shelf full of dried herbs and a genuine healing practice.

Walk into the woods with this awareness, and you'll notice things you've missed before. The way certain plants seem to lean toward you, offering themselves. How others withdraw, their energy turning inward, telling you this isn't the right time or place. Some practitioners call this *listening to the green world*—a skill our ancestors cultivated with the same care they gave to prayer. When you recognize that each root, leaf, and blossom carries its own spiritual essence, wildcrafting becomes an act of profound respect rather than mere extraction.

The mountains themselves will teach you this truth if you're patient. Spend time sitting quietly among the wild things. Notice how the land speaks through sensation, through sudden knowing, through the quality of silence that settles around a particular patch of yarrow or comfrey. This is the spiritual foundation of mountain medicine—the recognition that healing power flows not just from a plant's chemical compounds, but from its living spirit, willingly shared with those who approach in humility and faith.

Rituals of Permission and Gratitude

When you reach toward a plant, you're crossing a threshold. You're asking something alive to give up part of itself for your purpose. In the old ways, this wasn't something done carelessly. Permission and gratitude weren't polite additions to the work—they were the work itself, as essential as knowing which root to harvest or when the moon was right.

Asking permission means exactly that. Before your hand touches leaf or stem, you pause. You address the plant directly, out loud or in the quiet of your mind, stating your need clearly. "I'm here for medicine to ease fever," you might say, or "I need protection for my home." This isn't symbolic theater. You're genuinely requesting cooperation from a conscious being, and sometimes the answer is no. You'll feel it—a sense of wrongness, a sudden chill, an inexplicable reluctance in your own body. When that happens, you move on. The mountains hold abundance enough that refusal never means deprivation, only redirection.

Gratitude completes the exchange.

Traditional practitioners often left tobacco, cornmeal, or whiskey poured at the plant's base. These weren't random choices but substances their culture valued, making the offering a genuine sacrifice rather than an empty gesture. What you leave matters less than the sincerity behind it. A few coins, a strand of your own hair, water from your well—anything given with true appreciation honors the reciprocity at the heart of this practice. The offering acknowledges that you've received something precious and that the balance must be maintained.

This exchange operates on spiritual logic that strengthens everything that follows. Plants gathered with permission carry different energy than those yanked thoughtlessly from the ground. Practitioners who've worked both ways report the difference in potency—teas that work more powerfully, charms that hold their charge longer, salves that heal with unusual speed. The plant's spirit collaborates when you've approached with respect, lending its full power to your purpose.

Without that cooperation, you're working with dead matter rather than living medicine.

Never take more than a third from any plant or patch. This practical rule ensures the plant survives and regenerates, but it's also spiritual protocol—a way of demonstrating that your need doesn't override the plant's right to continued existence. Greed breaks relationship, and relationship is where the magic lives. When you gather with reverence, you're not just collecting herbs. You're entering into a sacred partnership that transforms both the medicine and the practitioner.

Harmony with the Land

Working against the land's rhythms is like trying to swim upstream in a flash flood. You'll exhaust yourself, gather poor medicine, and damage the places you need most. The mountains operate on cycles older than human memory, and aligning your practice with those rhythms isn't optional—it's the difference between magic that works and ritual that accomplishes nothing.

Seasonal timing matters profoundly. Spring growth carries different energy than autumn's retreat. Ginseng roots are traditionally harvested in the fall, when the plant draws its energy downward for winter dormancy, yielding a higher concentration of active compounds. Similarly, nettle leaves gathered in late spring, brimming with the plant's initial surge of growth, offer a distinct vitality compared to the mature, less potent leaves of August. Traditional practitioners tracked these cycles with precision because their families' health depended on effective medicine.

But seasonal knowledge represents only the surface.

The land speaks through subtler signs—drought stress that makes certain plants too fragile for harvest, unexpected abundance in a particular hollow, the early blooming that signals shifting conditions. When you attune yourself to these messages, you begin noticing what the mountain offers freely and what it's struggling to maintain. Sustainable gathering becomes intuitive rather than calculated. You feel when a patch needs rest the way you feel when your own body needs sleep.

This attunement amplifies your spiritual work in ways that sound mystical but operate practically. Plants gathered when they're thriving, from land that's balanced and healthy, carry stronger energy. The medicine reflects the vitality of its source. Conversely, harvesting from depleted areas produces depleted results, no matter how correctly you perform the ritual elements. Your magic draws power from the same source the plants do—the living land itself.

Practitioners who ignore these rhythms find their work weakening over time. Charms lose potency. Healing teas produce diminishing effects. The relationship fractures because it's become extractive rather than reciprocal. The land stops cooperating when you stop listening, and no amount of perfect technique compensates for that broken trust.

Pay attention to what's actually growing where you walk. Notice which plants return year after year and which disappear. Let abundance guide your gathering rather than forcing the land to provide what it's clearly struggling to sustain. This awareness isn't just ecological responsibility—it's the foundation of magic that continues working across decades rather than guttering out after initial success.

* * *

Techniques for Conscious Plant Gathering

Preparing the Mind and Spirit

Preparing for conscious plant gathering begins days before you step into the forest, not minutes. The work happens in the stillness of your own space, where you clarify intention with the same precision you'd use for any other spiritual undertaking. Sit quietly and ask yourself: What am I gathering, and for what specific purpose? Vague wants produce vague results. If you need red clover for protection work, say that—internally or aloud—until the purpose settles into your bones as certainty rather than hope.

Meditation before gathering isn't about reaching mystical transcendence. It's about clearing the mental noise that prevents you from hearing what the land communicates. Find twenty minutes the night before your harvest and sit with your intention, breathing it into focus until gathering feels less like a project and more like keeping an appointment with something alive. Some practitioners light a candle and speak their need three times. Others sit in silence until they feel an internal shift—a quieting that signals readiness.

Setting intention means declaring your purpose to the unseen forces that govern growth and decay.

This happens at your altar if you keep one, or simply standing at your threshold facing the direction you'll travel. State what you're gathering, why you need it, and what you're willing to offer in return. The formula matters less than sincerity, but the act of declaration matters profoundly—it transforms casual harvesting into formal request.

Physical preparation follows the spiritual. Bring clean tools, a basket or cloth bag rather than plastic, and whatever offering you've committed to leave. Tobacco remains traditional, but honey, cornmeal, or even pure water given with genuine gratitude serves the same function. Some practitioners fast the morning of gathering, arriving hungry to remind themselves they're petitioning rather than demanding. Others bathe in salt water to clear residual energy that might interfere with perception.

Before you touch a single leaf, stand at the forest's edge and announce yourself. This isn't theatrical—it's courtesy extended to conscious territory. Enter slowly, paying attention to whether the woods feel welcoming or resistant. That sensation in your gut when something feels wrong? Trust it completely.

Reading Nature's Signs

The land speaks before you ever touch a plant, but only if you're paying attention to the signals most gatherers ignore. Watch where birds congregate in the early morning—they know which clearings hold the strongest growth, and their presence often marks areas of balanced energy worth investigating. When crows gather near a patch of mullein but won't land, I've learned to move on. Something's off, whether depleted soil or spiritual exhaustion the plant can't mask.

Weather patterns tell you when gathering will succeed or fail. A sudden cold snap after warm days concentrates essential oils in roots and barks, making them exponentially more potent. Light rain the night before harvest softens earth without waterlogging plants, allowing clean extraction that honors root systems. Heavy storms preceding your gathering day signal postponement—not inconvenience, but direct communication that conditions aren't right. I once ignored this, harvesting ginseng during a warm spell following hard freeze. The roots crumbled like chalk, spiritually and physically depleted. The weather had told me to wait; I didn't listen.

Animal behavior provides the most precise guidance available if you develop eyes for it. Deer browsing heavily on a particular stand of plants indicates either scarcity elsewhere or exceptional vitality worth investigating—follow their judgment. Conversely, abundant growth completely untouched by any creature suggests toxicity or spiritual depletion that makes the plant unsuitable for healing work regardless of appearance. Research published in *Environmental Pollution* observed that European hares exhibited altered feeding patterns, actively avoiding vegetation in areas with high concentrations of heavy metals like lead and zinc, which can make plants unpalatable or toxic to them. This behavior provided crucial insights into plant suitability, offering information that might not be immediately apparent from visual inspection alone.

Insect activity matters too, though subtly.

Bees working a flowering plant signal peak vitality and proper timing. Absence of any insects around otherwise healthy growth raises questions worth investigating. These aren't superstitions but observable patterns connecting you to intelligence already operating in the ecosystem. The woods possess diagnostic systems more sophisticated than any you'll develop independently. Your role isn't mastering nature but learning to read what's already being communicated through flight patterns, feeding behaviors, and atmospheric shifts that precede your arrival by hours or days.

The Art of Asking Permission

Seeking consent begins the moment you identify what you need, not when your hand reaches the stem. Stand before the plant—don't crouch over it—and speak aloud. Silent thoughts lack the commitment required for genuine exchange. I say: "I come asking permission to take your leaves for healing work. If you're willing, show me." Then I wait, hand near but not touching, feeling for response.

The answer arrives as bodily sensation more than thought. Consent feels like warmth spreading through your palm, a subtle pull forward, or unexpected ease when you finally touch the stem. Refusal manifests as resistance—your hand hesitates despite intention, nausea rises without cause, or the plant seems to shrink back though no wind moves it. These aren't metaphors. Your body registers spiritual communication before your mind interprets it, which is why you can't rush this moment or fake attentiveness.

I've stood before perfect specimens of goldenseal, asked permission, and felt unmistakable no. I left empty-handed because consent withdrawn is relationship honored.

Traditional prayers vary by family and region, but effectiveness depends on specificity, not poetry. "Tobacco for your roots, healing for my daughter's cough that won't break"—this works. Vague gratitude doesn't. You're establishing terms of exchange, and both parties need clarity about what's being asked and what's being offered. My grandmother used Psalm 104 before gathering, emphasizing verses about herbs for service. Her sister poured whiskey at the base and recited no formal prayer, just clear statement of need and thanks. Both approaches succeeded because both were genuine.

The offering itself carries weight beyond symbolism. Tobacco remains traditional because it held genuine value as a sacred plant in many Indigenous cultures across the Americas. Cornmeal works because it nourishes—you're returning something useful, not disposing of trash. Coins feel transactional and rarely produce the energetic shift that signals accepted exchange. I've seen practitioners leave crystals, which strikes me as self-important. The land doesn't need your quartz; it needs reciprocity it recognizes as sacrifice.

Where consent practice fails: treating it as performance rather than negotiation.

You cannot mime respect and expect results. If you're gathering in a hurry, speaking words while thinking about your car idling on the logging road, the plant knows. Your work will be weak, or worse, the land stops answering entirely. This happens to practitioners who start strong but let busyness erode genuine presence, and rebuilding that trust takes months of offerings without asking anything in return.

Offering Gratitude and Reciprocity

Reciprocity doesn't end when the plant enters your basket. What you do after gathering determines whether the relationship continues or collapses into extraction.

I return within a week to the same patch, even if it requires extra travel. Bring water during drought—a full gallon poured slowly around remaining plants, not a token splash. Pull invasive species choking the area. Clear fallen branches blocking light. This isn't symbolic maintenance; it's literal care for the community you just took from. The land remembers who tends and who simply takes.

Propagation completes the exchange in ways offerings alone cannot. If you harvested roots, scatter seeds from the mature plant before you leave. Plant three saplings the following spring within a mile of your gathering site. I keep cloth bags of seeds from every plant I work with regularly, collected during abundance and stored until needed. Goldenseal, ginseng, black cohosh—these slow-growing medicines require years to mature, so replacing what you take isn't optional if you want the patch available for your grandchildren.

Some practitioners maintain what I call reciprocity sites: wild areas they tend without harvesting, offering labor as thanks for medicines taken elsewhere. You might spend an afternoon clearing trash from a creek that feeds wetlands where you gather skullcap, or removing tree-of-heaven seedlings threatening native understory. This demonstrates to the land that your relationship extends beyond need. The spirits notice who shows up when they want nothing.

Document what you take and what you give back. I maintain a gathering journal with harvest dates, amounts taken, offerings left, and restoration work completed. This prevents over-harvesting through forgetfulness and reveals patterns—which patches recover quickly, which need longer rest, where abundance increases after tending.

When a patch dies despite careful harvesting, don't simply find another. Drought, disease, deer pressure, or disrupted mycelial networks all require different responses. Sometimes the land is asking you to let that medicine rest for years. Honoring that request, even when inconvenient, builds trust that opens other doors. The mountain provides, but only to those who prove they understand the difference between partnership and plunder.

* * *

Enhancing Magic with Sacred Wildcrafting

Spiritual Preparation and Mindset

Three days before you enter the forest, begin your preparation with silence. Not forced meditation or elaborate ritual, but simply sitting still for ten minutes each morning without reaching for your phone or filling the quiet with mental chatter. This creates the receptive state necessary for genuine communication with the land. Your mind needs to remember how to listen before spirits have anything to say to you.

On the second day, write your intention on paper. Not what you think sounds mystical, but what you actually need: "I'm gathering mullein to ease my daughter's cough" or "I need yarrow to stop bleeding when I'm working alone on the property." Speak it aloud three times—once at dawn, once at midday, once at dusk. Each repetition builds certainty, and certainty is what plants respond to.

The night before gathering, prepare your offering and announce your plan at your threshold. Stand at your front door after dark, facing outward, and state clearly: "Tomorrow I'm entering the forest to gather [specific plant]. I'm bringing [specific offering]. I ask permission and promise reciprocity." This isn't theater. You're formally requesting access to conscious territory, and spirits mark whether you actually show up with what you promised.

On gathering day, assemble these items before you leave: a clean blade you've used only for plant work, a basket or cloth bag, your offering in a small pouch, and a notebook. *Clean* means ritually washed the night before—hold your knife under cold running water while stating your intention. Physical tools carry energetic residue from previous use. A knife that's gutted fish or opened Amazon packages brings that energy into sacred exchange.

At the forest's edge, stop and announce yourself. Say your name, state your purpose, show your offering. Wait thirty seconds in actual silence—count if you must—and notice what your body tells you. Tightness in your chest or sudden urge to leave means the land's saying no, and you honor that by returning another day. A sense of ease or forward pull means proceed, but stay alert. Consent isn't permanent; conditions change as you move deeper.

When you find your plant, conduct this abbreviated protocol if you're pressed for time: kneel, place your hand near the base without touching, speak your specific need aloud, wait for bodily response. Yes feels like warmth or gentle magnetic pull. No feels like withdrawal, cold, or your hand naturally pulling back. Take only from plants that consent, never more than one-third of what's visible, and leave your offering at the root base immediately after cutting (Wildfoods 4 Wildlife, n.d.; Boye, 2024).

Failures look like this: harvesting while mentally planning dinner, taking because the plant's convenient rather than willing, offering tobacco you don't actually value, skipping the waiting period because you're certain you felt consent. If you recognize yourself in any of these, course-correct immediately. The work requires discipline.

Return within seven days to water the patch if weather's been dry, or to remove the invasive honeysuckle choking nearby saplings. Reciprocity isn't metaphor. The land remembers who keeps their word and who takes without giving back.

Your first three gathering expeditions will feel awkward and possibly foolish. That discomfort is your skepticism dying, which needs to happen before the work becomes real. Push through it. The spirits are patient with genuine seekers, less so with those who abandon the practice at the first hint of uncertainty.

Translating Communion into Potency

The transformative shift doesn't arrive overnight when you begin sacred wildcrafting. During your early weeks, you'll find yourself kneeling beside yarrow or mullein, speaking requests that feel clumsy in your mouth, leaving small offerings of cornmeal or tobacco that might seem like playacting. You'll walk home carrying your gathered plants, uncertain whether anything of spiritual significance actually occurred. This awkward beginning is where everyone starts.

Sacred wildcrafting builds its power through accumulation, not epiphany. The forest doesn't announce its acceptance of you with thunder or vision. Instead, the relationship deepens through quiet repetition until you notice, perhaps months into your practice, that the land feels different beneath your feet. You begin perceiving subtle communications you previously missed—the way certain plants seem to lean toward you while others pull back, how the quality of light shifts when you've gathered enough, the distinct feeling in your chest that signals permission or refusal.

Each conscious choice reinforces the spiritual current flowing between you and the green world. When you pause to request consent instead of simply harvesting, you're teaching your deeper senses to recognize the plant's response. That faint warmth in your palms, the sudden certainty, the inexplicable reluctance—these become your vocabulary of communication. The offerings you leave at root level create energetic exchange rather than spiritual debt. You take, yes, but you also give, maintaining the balance that keeps wildcrafting sacred rather than merely extractive.

The plants gathered through spiritual communion carry a fundamentally different medicine than those taken without acknowledgment. When you approach a stand of boneset with reverence, stating your need and waiting for response, the plant material you ultimately gather becomes infused with intentional power. This isn't metaphor or wishful thinking. Your healing teas become more effective. Your protection bundles hold stronger charge. The salves you prepare from consciously gathered roots work more reliably because they contain not just chemical constituents but also the spiritual agreement between you and the plant's essence.

This is why two identical remedies—same plant, same preparation method, same proportions—can yield vastly different results. The remedy crafted from plants gathered as spiritual communion carries the imprint of that relationship, the blessing exchanged in the moment of harvest. Faith transforms gathering into partnership, and partnership amplifies magic beyond what technique alone can achieve.

CHAPTER 5

Secret 4: Building Powerful Protection Through Layered Charms And Spiritual Fortification

---

The Foundations of Protective Magic in Appalachian Tradition

Historical Roots of Protection

Archaeological findings and historical accounts reveal instances where Appalachian families deliberately embedded protective items within their homes. Researchers have documented discoveries of witch bottles containing pins, hair, and sometimes urine, or caches of iron nails, silver coins, and packets of specific herbs, hidden in walls or under hearths of older dwellings. These layered defenses were often added over generations, addressing various threats from illness and misfortune to perceived malevolent spiritual forces, reflecting a practical spiritual engineering developed across generations of mountain isolation.

Appalachian protective magic emerged from necessity in an environment where formal law enforcement barely existed and medical help might be days away. Families required *immediate, reliable defense* against both physical dangers and spiritual threats that settlers,

Cherokee communities, and African Americans all recognized as genuine.

The foundation rested on a profound convergence of defensive traditions. Scottish settlers brought knowledge of threshold protections and iron's power against malevolent forces. Cherokee practitioners understood how specific plants could create spiritual barriers and how land itself possessed protective qualities when approached correctly. African spiritual technologies contributed sophisticated layering techniques—the understanding that multiple defenses working simultaneously created exponential rather than additive power.

Christianity didn't replace these practices but strengthened them through biblical authority. Psalm 91 became a shield when written on paper and hidden in walls. The cross functioned as both religious symbol and geometric power, its four points creating spiritual boundaries. This wasn't theological contradiction but strategic accumulation, where practitioners combined every available defensive resource because survival demanded it.

Historical trauma intensified these traditions. Communities facing persecution, land theft, and violence developed protection methods born from real and present danger, creating a magical practice as robust and enduring as the mountains themselves.

Symbolic Tools and Materials

Salt stands as the most fundamental barrier material in Appalachian protective work. Its preservative qualities translate directly into spiritual preservation, preventing decay of protective energy and creating boundaries that malevolent forces cannot cross. Mountain practitioners line windowsills, sprinkle thresholds, and cast circles with salt because it simultaneously purifies space and establishes definitive spiritual territory.

The substance costs little, requires no preparation, and works immediately—critical factors when protection couldn't wait for elaborate ritual.

Iron carries different power entirely. Its presence disrupts negative spiritual energy through magnetic interference, quite literally scrambling harmful intentions before they can take root.

Horseshoes above doors, iron nails driven into doorframes, and cast-iron skillets placed beneath beds all serve the same purpose: creating electromagnetic disturbance that spiritual threats cannot navigate. The tradition recognizes iron as spiritually *disorienting*, a material so fundamentally opposed to ethereal manipulation that its mere presence provides defense.

Herbs function as the third essential category, though their application differs markedly from salt's boundaries or iron's disruption. Plants like angelica root, devil's shoestring, and rue carry protective virtues that must be *activated* through faith and intention. These aren't passive barriers but living allies whose spiritual properties respond to the practitioner's belief. Devil's shoestring tangles negative influences, quite literally tripping up harmful energy.

Rue breaks curses through its bitter essence. Angelica root calls upon divine protection, its very name invoking heavenly guardianship.

Each material represents not just physical substance but concentrated spiritual purpose—tools that work because generations of mountain practitioners have imbued them with tested power and unwavering faith.

Rituals and Spoken Incantations

Materials alone accomplish nothing without the spoken word to direct their power. Appalachian protective magic lives in the practitioner's voice—in whispered prayers over salt lines, in forceful declarations that establish spiritual boundaries, in the measured cadence of biblical verses transformed into incantations. Words carry intention into manifestation, giving shapeless belief concrete form that the invisible world recognizes and respects.

Traditional practitioners understood that certain phrases accumulated power through repetition across generations. Psalm 91 became the cornerstone of mountain protection work (Long, 2012) not through arbitrary choice but through proven results—families who spoke these verses over their homes weathered spiritual storms that destroyed their neighbors' peace (Long, 2012). The words themselves became *charged*, carrying the accumulated faith of countless believers who staked their safety on this specific invocation.

Timing determines whether spoken protection takes root or dissipates uselessly into air.

Protective rituals demand alignment with natural cycles that amplify spiritual work. The waning moon dissolves unwanted influences, making it ideal for banishing and boundary-setting. Dawn carries fresh energy perfect for establishing new protections, while dusk transitions into the liminal hours when the veil thins and words spoken carry double weight. Mountain practitioners didn't perform protection work randomly but watched the sky, tracked the moon's phases, and chose their moments with tactical precision. A salt line laid at midnight during the dark moon functions fundamentally differently than one scattered carelessly at noon—the former draws upon the concentrated power of absence and boundary, while the latter fights against the sun's expansive, dissolving energy.

Yet all the proper materials, perfectly timed rituals, and traditional words mean nothing without the practitioner's unshakeable faith. This isn't religious doctrine but operational requirement—protective magic works because the practitioner believes it works with such certainty that doubt cannot enter. That conviction transforms ordinary salt into spiritual barrier, common speech into incantation, and simple gesture into forcefield. Without it, practitioners merely go through motions, creating theater instead of protection.

* * *

Crafting and Empowering Layered Charms

Selecting Symbolic Materials

Materials in Appalachian protection work carry dual identity—they function both as physical substances with measurable properties and as spiritual collaborators with distinct personalities and purposes. This isn't metaphor or poetic interpretation. When a practitioner selects a piece of hematite for grounding work, she's engaging with iron's ancient relationship to blood, earth's magnetic field, and the stone's capacity to literally pull scattered energy downward into coherent form.

Herbs demonstrate this principle most clearly because their chemical constituents provide tangible evidence of spiritual function. Rue contains compounds, such as 2-undecanone, that genuinely repel insects, which mountain practitioners understood as physical proof of its energetic boundary-setting properties. The plant that keeps pests away also deflects unwanted spiritual intrusions. Salt crystallizes in perfect geometric patterns because it organizes molecular chaos into structure—the same organizing force we invoke when we lay salt lines across doorways. The material world and the spirit world aren't separate realms requiring translation; they're *continuous expressions* of the same underlying forces. (Paluch et al., 2021)

Metals carry memory in their molecular structure. Iron forged in mountain smithies absorbed the intentions of makers, the prayers whispered over anvils, the sweat and blood of those who shaped it. A hand-wrought nail driven into a doorframe for protection brings not just iron's traditional association with warding, but the specific history embedded in its physical form. Silver tarnishes in the presence of sulfur compounds, giving us a visible indicator of environmental change—a sensitivity we recognize as spiritual discernment.

Stones speak in slower rhythms. Their formation required millennia of pressure, heat, and transformation. When you hold river-smoothed quartz, you're touching hundreds of thousands of years of water's patient shaping. That endurance becomes part of your charm's foundation. The energetic properties aren't imposed by belief; they emerge from authentic engagement with what the material has experienced and become.

The key lies in *recognition* rather than assignment. You don't give materials their power—you acknowledge what's already present.

Weaving Intent with Knot Magic

In 1989, folklorist Gerald Milnes documented a protective working performed by an 87-year-old practitioner named Cora Adkins in Braxton County, West Virginia. Her grandson faced persistent harassment from a neighbor who'd threatened violence three times in as many weeks. Local law enforcement had proved useless. Cora worked a nine-knot charm using red thread and a psalm she'd learned from her grandmother.

She tied the first knot at dawn on a Saturday, speaking the opening line of Psalm 37 as she pulled it tight: *"Fret not thyself because of evildoers."* Each subsequent knot received the next verse, tied at the same hour over nine consecutive days. She worked with deliberate slowness, treating each motion as sacred act rather than mechanical repetition. The thread went into a flannel pouch with devil's shoestring and salt, then into the grandson's truck.

The neighbor stopped his harassment within a week.

More significantly, he moved away within three months. Cora attributed the success not to the specific psalm or the red thread—though both mattered—but to the binding action itself. Each knot captured intention the way a jar captures air, creating discrete containers of focused will.

Knot magic operates on elegant simplicity: the physical act of tying mirrors the spiritual act of securing. When you pull thread tight, you're demonstrating exactly what you want spiritual forces to do with your intention—hold it fixed, prevent its unraveling, keep it constant despite external pressure. The number of knots establishes rhythm and creates relationship. Three knots invoke the Trinity and represent beginning, middle, and completion. Seven knots align with biblical perfection and the traditional power number across multiple spiritual traditions. Nine knots multiply three by three, creating exponential rather than additive force.

The material of the cord matters as much as the number. Cotton absorbs and holds. Silk conducts energy smoothly. Wool brings animal vitality, and hemp resists decay. Between each knot lives the space where power accumulates—the *potential* before the next securing. That tension creates the charm's actual architecture.

Empowering Charms with Spoken Words

Words spoken with conviction carry force that silent intention cannot match. Your voice moves air, creates vibration, physically alters the space around your working—but more critically, vocalization demands precision that thought alone permits you to avoid. When you speak a charm aloud, vagueness becomes immediately obvious. Mumbled uncertainty sounds nothing like focused command.

The most effective incantations in Appalachian tradition weren't borrowed wholesale from grimoires. They emerged from practitioners who understood their own spiritual vocabulary—the phrases that carried weight in their personal cosmology, whether biblical verses absorbed from childhood, fragments of hymns, or declarations formed from direct experience. A practiced Catholic might invoke specific saints with genuine authority. A Baptist-raised practitioner channels more power through scriptural language than through unfamiliar Gaelic phrases, regardless of their historical authenticity.

Personalization doesn't mean invention from nothing.

Start with proven structures, then make them yours through sustained use. Take Psalm 91, a foundational element of Appalachian protection work (Richards, 2021). Speaking it word-for-word carries accumulated power from generations of prior use. But speaking it until specific phrases *resonate*—until certain lines feel charged when they leave your mouth—transforms rote recitation into genuine incantation. You might find yourself returning repeatedly to "He shall cover thee with his feathers" while other verses pass with less intensity. That's your spiritual signature emerging. (Richards, 2021)

Rhythm matters as much as content. Words work most powerfully when spoken at the pace of steady heartbeat, each syllable given full weight. Rushed words scatter intention. Dragged-out phrases lose momentum before completion. You're looking for the cadence that feels inevitable, like water finding its course downhill.

Yet spoken charms fail reliably under specific conditions: when practitioners read them like shopping lists, when self-consciousness produces performance rather than declaration, when doubt creeps into the voice itself through hesitation or rising inflection that transforms statement into question. The charm must land with finality. If you can't speak your words with unwavering conviction, the materials you've assembled remain just objects in a bag.

Rituals for Activation and Maintenance

Activation isn't permanent. An untended charm loses potency like a fading relationship—not suddenly, but through gradual disconnection. Materials stay physically intact, but their spiritual charge dissipates, especially in protective environments. A mojo bag absorbing negative energy for months becomes saturated, its capacity exhausted.

Begin recharging during the waning moon, when thinning energy facilitates clearing accumulated interference before rebuilding protection. Remove the charm. If it contains perishable elements like herbs, examine them for deterioration. Crushed or moldy materials require replacement—not due to folklore, but because decay signals spiritual depletion beyond verbal restoration.

Pass the charm through smoke from burning sage or cedar, moving it deliberately through the ascending column. This is not merely symbolic. The smoke's rising energy lifts stagnant accumulation from the materials, creating receptivity for renewed charge.

Speak your original intention again, but don't merely repeat previous words. State what the charm has accomplished: "You have held this threshold against harm. You have turned back ill will." Acknowledgment matters. Then declare its continued purpose with present-tense certainty, using the exact phrasing that carried power during initial creation.

For charms protecting specific locations, physical reconnection strengthens renewal. Press the mojo bag against its guarded doorframe. Hold the bottle charm against its windowsill. Let your hands bridge renewed intention directly into both object and protected space.

Some practitioners anoint recharged charms with protection oil—preferably homemade from herbs gathered with permission. Three drops suffice. Others add a single fresh element: a new iron nail, a pinch of recently harvested rue, or salt blessed that morning.

Return the charm to its position before the new moon, timing final placement for dawn when establishing energies run strongest. The interval between clearing and replacement allows spiritual reset—emptiness that permits fuller recharging than continuous occupation.

Charms under constant stress benefit from monthly attention. Quarterly renewal suffices for most household protections. Ultimately, trust your direct perception over arbitrary schedules.

* * *

Spiritual Fortification: Strengthening Protection with Intent and Ritual

Harnessing Intent in Rituals

Before constructing any protective charm, spend three full minutes stilling your mind completely. This isn't meditation in the modern sense —it's deliberate emptying that creates space for focused will to form without interference. Sit with your materials spread before you. Close your eyes. Count nine breaths, each slower than the last, until mental chatter recedes and you feel the weight of your body against the chair.

Now speak your intention aloud once, precisely. Not "I want protection" but "This charm guards my threshold against malicious intent and spiritual intrusion." The specificity matters. Vague intent dissipates like morning fog; clear directives consolidate power into narrow channels that penetrate deeper into the spiritual realm. Your words become anchors.

As you work—knotting thread, binding herbs, inscribing symbols —hold that singular intention like a burning coal in your mind's eye. Every movement should echo it. When you tie the third knot, you're not merely fastening string; you're *binding protection* into physical form through the force of your concentrated will. The charm becomes a vessel for your spiritual energy, amplified by the clarity of your purpose.

End each ritual with gratitude spoken to the spirits who aid your work and the divine source that empowers it. This isn't courtesy—it's spiritual fortification. Gratitude completes the circuit of energy, sealing your intention within the charm and strengthening the protective barrier you've woven. The ritual doesn't end when your hands stop moving; it ends when you've honored the sacred exchange between your faith, your materials, and the unseen forces that answer your call.

Symbolism in Protective Rituals

Grounding your protection work requires fluency in the symbols that carry power through generations of mountain practice. Each mark functions as concentrated spiritual language, speaking directly to forces that respond to visual directive more readily than scattered intention.

Start with the cross. Not merely Christian iconography, but a pervasive protective symbol in Appalachian work—representing four directions secured, with vertical and horizontal forces balanced. Folk practitioners often draw it over doorways with blessed oil, carve it into wooden protection charms, or trace it in salt across thresholds. The motion matters as much as the result: top to bottom establishes divine connection, left to right seals earthly boundary. When you trace a cross, you're not simply making a shape—you're invoking the alignment of heaven and earth, creating a fortified intersection where malevolent forces find no passage.

The protective knot carries significant weight in our tradition. (aromaG's Botanica, 2021)

Interlocking threads or lines represent intentions bound into permanent form, spiritual agreements made tangible through deliberate weaving.

When you craft a knot with protective intent, each crossing seals your purpose tighter, each loop captures and holds the energy you're directing. Traditional practitioners work these knots into charm bags, embroider them onto clothing hems, or carve their patterns into wood. The complexity of the knot often reflects the layered nature of the protection desired—simple overhand knots for basic warding, elaborate Celtic-influenced patterns for more comprehensive spiritual fortification.

The pentacle appears throughout Appalachian protection work, though its presence surprises those who view mountain magic through a purely Christian lens (Grove and Grotto, 2017). This five-pointed star enclosed in a circle predates Christianity, carried here through Celtic memory and integrated seamlessly into folk practice. Each point represents an element—earth, air, fire, water, spirit—contained and balanced within the protective circle. Draw it point-up for invoking protection, trace it in the air before entering uncertain spaces, inscribe it on protective talismans to create a complete spiritual shield that acknowledges all forces of creation working in harmony.

Ritual Timing and Environment

Protection work collapses when practitioners ignore timing. Conducting rituals during energetically hostile conditions creates charms that feel hollow, their power dissipated before it ever settles. Working protection during the full moon when you need waning energy to banish creates spiritual contradiction—like planting seeds in frozen ground and expecting harvest. The waning moon carries the energy of release, banishing, and clearing away what no longer serves. The full moon amplifies and brings things to fruition. The moon pulls tides and blood; it shapes when magic takes root (Cunningham, 1985). (Telesco, 2020).

If your charm feels inert, examine what phase you worked it under.

Environmental contamination undermines even the most carefully constructed work. Conducting protection rituals in spaces saturated with conflict, digital interference, or simple clutter creates noise that drowns your focused intention. Your protection charm absorbs the ambient chaos rather than your directed purpose. The solution isn't complex: clear the space first.

Remove electronics. Clean physically. Burn purifying herbs like sage or cedar to lift stagnant energy. If the space can't be cleared—apartment living, shared homes—create a temporary sacred boundary using salt lines or intentional candle placement. Small, purified space works better than large, contaminated area. (Malhotra, 2021)

Weak verbal formulation produces weak results. Practitioners speak incantations with uncertainty, their voice trailing upward into questions rather than landing as commands. Words mumbled or rushed carry no weight. When protection fails, speak your incantation aloud right now and listen honestly to your delivery. Does it sound like you believe what you're saying? Recovery means rewriting the charm in language that feels true in your mouth—whether that's biblical verse, simple declaration, or rhythmic repetition. Then practice speaking it with your full chest, each syllable deliberate, until the words themselves feel like physical construction.

Material incompatibility happens when practitioners follow instructions without understanding function. Using lavender in aggressive banishment because "herbs are good" misses the point entirely. Iron carries strong protective and grounding qualities, but its specific properties may not suit all needs. If your protection isn't holding, examine whether your materials match your actual need. Replace components thoughtfully, letting function guide selection rather than availability or aesthetic preference.

Integrating Ancestral Wisdom

When protection fails despite correct materials and timing, the missing element is often ancestral support. Many practitioners work as isolated individuals, attempting to generate spiritual power from personal will alone. But you're not the first person in your lineage to need protection—your grandmother knew how to keep harm from the threshold. Her grandmother before that survived circumstances you can barely imagine. Their accumulated spiritual strength remains available when you establish deliberate connection.

Start with the physical.

Create a dedicated space—shelf, small table, corner of your bedroom—where ancestors can gather. Place photographs if you have them. If not, use objects that carry family memory: inherited jewelry, tools, handwritten letters, anything touched by those who came before. Add a white candle, a glass of fresh water changed weekly, and simple offerings: coffee if they drank it, tobacco, a portion of meals you cook. This becomes your ancestral altar, the meeting place between your protective work and their enduring wisdom.

Speak to them regularly, not in formal prayer but direct conversation. Tell them what threatens your household. Ask specifically for their protection to join yours. *"Grandma, I'm working protection for this house. I need your help keeping my children safe."* Name them if you can. The specificity matters—vague appeals to "ancestors" carry less weight than addressing the grandmother who raised six children through the Depression, who absolutely knew how to fortify a home against danger.

Before working your next protection charm, light the candle at your ancestral space. Invite them into the work itself, acknowledging that their strength supplements yours. As you construct the charm, feel their presence as additional hands steadying your own.

This isn't metaphor. Practitioners report physical sensations: warmth, pressure at the shoulders, sudden clarity about which materials to use. Not everyone receives dramatic signs. Sometimes ancestral support feels like quiet confidence, the absence of the doubt that previously undermined your work.

Protection charms created with ancestral collaboration hold longer, recover faster from saturation, and carry authority beyond individual capacity. You're building on foundation they already laid, adding one more layer to spiritual fortification that spans generations. That accumulated power changes everything.

CHAPTER 6

Secret 5: Folk Healing Remedies That Blend Plant Wisdom With Spiritual Intention

---

The Spiritual Properties of Healing Plants

Plant Spirits and Ancestral Knowledge

When a mountain healer first approached bloodroot with open hands and a quiet heart, the plant didn't speak in words. Instead, warmth spread through weathered fingers, and knowledge arrived whole—how to harvest without wounding, where to cut, when to wait. This isn't quaint storytelling. It's the living reality of practitioners who understand that plants carry consciousness, memory, and deliberate intention, making them allies in healing rather than ingredients to be extracted.

To work with plant spirits, you must release the notion that herbs are merely chemical compounds waiting to be processed. Take yellowroot, thriving along creek banks with its characteristic bitter taste. The plant doesn't just contain berberine—it embodies the cool darkness of mountain streams, the persistence of roots gripping stone, and generations of healing wisdom flowing through its yellow fibers. When a healer addresses yellowroot directly, seeking permission before the first cut, the resulting medicine operates on frequencies beyond the physical. The botanical compounds work, yes, but so does the spiritual agreement between healer and plant.

Ancestral wisdom flows through these relationships with startling precision. Mullein's tall flowering stalk marks it as a boundary keeper, its leaves soft enough to line coffins yet strong enough to guard against malevolent spirits. Sassafras announces itself through scent alone—spicy, cleansing, undeniable—a plant that Native peoples recognized for purification long before European settlers arrived. This knowledge wasn't written in books. It was whispered plant to person, generation to generation, becoming part of the land's memory itself.

Certain plants stand as particularly powerful spirit allies in mountain tradition. Devil's shoestring tangles underfoot with roots that bind and trip, making it perfect for protection work—its physical form mirrors its spiritual function. Rue's bitter, penetrating scent doesn't just clear congested airways; it drives out attached energies with the same forceful clarity. These aren't symbolic associations we've invented. They're observed correspondences between what a plant *is* and what it *does* in both seen and unseen realms.

Understanding this transforms everything about healing work.

You're not extracting compounds from passive matter. You're entering into relationship with conscious beings who choose whether to lend their power. A plantain poultice applied with gratitude and clear intention draws poison differently than the same leaves crushed with distraction. The chemistry remains identical, but the spiritual collaboration either awakens or sleeps.

Learning to perceive plant consciousness demands a patience most modern souls have forgotten. You must sit with growing things until your thoughts quiet, your awareness expands beyond words, and subtle communications register as intuition, warmth in your palms, or sudden knowing that arrives complete. This is how the old ones learned. This is how the plants still teach, if we remember how to listen.

Vibrational Medicine and Energy Fields

Every plant hums with its own frequency—a subtle, sacred vibration that resonates through root and stem, leaf and flower. This isn't poetic fancy; it's the foundation of vibrational medicine, a concept woven deep into the fabric of mountain healing. When a granny woman reaches for yarrow or mullein, she's not just selecting a remedy based on chemical compounds. She's listening for the plant's energetic signature, feeling for the way its particular frequency might harmonize with a person's disrupted energy, coaxing the body back toward balance and wholeness.

Understanding this requires a shift in perspective. The body itself is not merely flesh and bone but a complex field of energy, constantly vibrating, constantly responding to the world around it. Illness, in this view, represents discord—a frequency gone awry, a pattern interrupted. Healing plants carry their own stable, coherent vibrations, and when introduced with intention and respect, they can act as tuning forks, helping to restore the body's natural rhythm.

Practitioners learn to attune themselves to these energies through quiet observation and deep listening. You might sit with a plant in the wild, allowing its presence to settle into your awareness. Some describe it as a tingling in the palms, others as a sense of warmth or coolness, still others as an intuitive knowing that blooms without words. This attunement isn't a one-time skill but a continuous practice of sensitivity, refined through seasons of respectful engagement with the green world.

When you align your intention with a plant's vibrational power, you're not commanding or extracting. You're entering into partnership. Your focused belief becomes the conduit through which the plant's energy can flow most effectively, directed toward the specific healing needed. This is where faith meets botany, where the spiritual and physical realms intertwine so completely that separating them would diminish both. The remedy you create carries not just the plant's physical properties but its energetic essence, amplified by your reverence and intention, ready to work its restoration on body and spirit alike.

Intention and Spiritual Activation

Belief in folk healing isn't passive acceptance. It's an active force that determines whether medicine truly works.

The mountain practitioners understood something modern culture has forgotten: the healer's conviction functions as the bridge between physical remedy and spiritual transformation. When doubt creeps into the preparation of a tincture or the speaking of a healing charm, it doesn't just weaken the work—it fundamentally alters the energetic imprint of what you're creating. Your uncertainty becomes embedded in the remedy itself, creating medicine that addresses symptoms without touching the deeper disharmony that needs healing.

This matters more than most practitioners realize.

Consider what happens when you gather elderberries with half-hearted intention, your mind wandering to grocery lists and obligations while your hands move mechanically through the motions. The berries you collect carry the same chemical compounds, yes, but they lack the *activation* that comes from focused spiritual attention. Conversely, when you approach the same elder tree with reverence, state your purpose clearly, and infuse every step of preparation with unwavering belief in the plant's power to heal, you're not just making syrup. You're creating a vessel for transformation, charged with your conviction and the plant's willing participation.

The old practitioners knew this intuitively. They wouldn't dream of preparing medicine while angry, distracted, or doubtful. They'd wait, sometimes for days, until their internal state aligned with the work at hand. This discipline wasn't superstition but practical recognition that the maker's energy saturates the medicine. Your emotional state, your level of certainty, your depth of connection to the plant spirit—all of these become ingredients as real as water or alcohol.

The stakes run higher than failed remedies, though that's consequence enough.

When you practice without genuine belief, you train yourself in hollow gestures rather than authentic power. You go through motions that might look identical to traditional practice but lack the spiritual substance that makes them effective. Over time, this creates a dangerous pattern where you disconnect from the living heart of the work, reducing sacred practice to recipe-following.

Evidence supports what grandmothers always knew. The widely documented placebo effect, where belief in a treatment itself can alleviate symptoms, clearly demonstrates the power of the mind over the body. Further research in psychoneuroimmunology highlights how psychological states, including positive expectation, can influence physiological processes and even immune function. All of this points toward the same truth—consciousness affects matter. Your focused belief doesn't just accompany the healing; it activates it.

* * *

The Power of Intention in Folk Healing

Understanding Energetic Intent

Intention in folk healing isn't some abstract spiritual theory floating in mountain mist. It's the active force that determines whether you're making tea or medicine.

When my grandmother prepared boneset tea for fever, she didn't merely follow steps. She held the dried leaves between her palms first, speaking directly to the plant's spirit, naming the person who needed healing, describing the fever's grip on their body. Her focused attention created a channel through which the plant's healing properties could flow with direction and purpose. The same boneset gathered by someone distracted, prepared while their mind wandered to yesterday's argument or tomorrow's chores, might reduce fever through chemical action alone—but it wouldn't carry the layered power of remedy made with complete spiritual presence.

Energetic intent functions as the organizing principle that directs botanical compounds toward specific healing outcomes. Plants contain multitudes: yarrow simultaneously stops bleeding, reduces fever, and soothes inflammation. Without clear intention, that scattered potential remains diffuse. With focused will, you're essentially instructing the plant which of its many medicines to emphasize, which vibrational frequency to amplify. This isn't controlling the plant—it's entering into precise collaboration. (Saad & Said, 2011) (Duke, 2002)

The difference manifests in tangible ways.

A salve for burns prepared with fierce protective intention while visualizing cooling relief and skin regenerating creates not just physical barrier but energetic shield. That same recipe made hastily, mind elsewhere, produces functional ointment without the spiritual activation that accelerates healing beyond chemistry alone. Recipients often report feeling the difference before rational explanation: one remedy brings immediate calm alongside physical relief, while the other simply treats symptoms.

This directional force requires more than positive thinking. True intention demands specificity—not vague hopes for "wellness" but clear vision of blocked energy releasing, inflammation subsiding, spirit returning to depleted body. It requires sustained focus throughout preparation, from the moment you reach for dried herbs until you seal the final jar. Most critically, it requires absolute conviction that your focused will, combined with plant intelligence, creates transformation.

The old practitioners understood this instinctively. They wouldn't let doubting hands touch healing work.

Aligning Mind, Body, and Spirit

The history of traditional healing, from Indigenous shamans to Ayurvedic *vaidyas*, consistently emphasizes that a practitioner's internal alignment profoundly impacts a remedy's efficacy. When healers are fragmented—distracted, fatigued, or emotionally unsettled—their preparations can carry this energetic incoherence. Imagine a traditional herbalist meticulously following ancestral recipes, but with a mind consumed by personal worries. Despite correct botanical ingredients, the medicine may lack its vital energetic charge, becoming like static interference and rendering the botanicals less potent. The remedy's true power, therefore, isn't solely in its physical components but in the resonant field of the one preparing it. Only when the practitioner achieves a state of clarity, single-pointed focus, and deep connection to the healing task can the remedy's full potential be transmitted, creating a palpable shift in the recipient's condition.

Alignment means your conscious intention, physical actions, and spiritual conviction move as unified current rather than competing streams.

When fragmented, you might speak healing words while your body tenses with doubt, or prepare remedy with correct movements while your mind rehearses worry. Each misalignment creates energetic contradiction that weakens the whole, like trying to pour water through a cracked vessel. The old mountain healers understood this intimately—they knew that divided attention produced divided results, no matter how perfectly the herbs were gathered or how precisely the proportions were measured.

Practical cultivation begins before you touch a single herb. Experienced practitioners establish what they call "coming to center"—deliberate stilling that synchronizes breath, settles racing thoughts, and grounds scattered energy back into present moment. Some use specific breathing patterns: four counts in, hold four, release four, creating rhythm that calms nervous system and focuses awareness. Others speak brief prayers that aren't religious performance but genuine centering—words that remind them of lineage, purpose, and the sacred nature of healing work they're entering. This threshold moment transforms preparation from mechanical task into spiritual act.

Physical preparation matters equally. You can't align fragmented energy while rushing. The old healers moved with deliberate slowness during remedy preparation, each gesture intentional rather than automatic. Measuring herbs became meditation. Stirring became prayer. Straining became blessing. This measured pace isn't inefficiency—it's the rhythm that allows complete presence to saturate every action, ensuring your full being participates rather than just your hands going through motions.

The cultivation never ends. Even practitioners with decades of experience check their alignment before beginning healing work, recognizing that yesterday's centeredness doesn't carry forward automatically. Each time you prepare remedy, you choose either fragmented efficiency or integrated power.

Creating Intentional Rituals

Ritual structure provides the container for focused intention, but only when that structure emerges from genuine need rather than borrowed templates. The most powerful healing rituals aren't elaborate performances with dozens of candles and memorized incantations. They're spare, personal acts where every element carries specific meaning for that healer working with that particular remedy for that exact purpose.

Think of the traditional mountain healer lighting a single candle while invoking the patient's name, stirring a preparation clockwise with focused visualization of wellness, sealing it with a heartfelt blessing.

These acts, though outwardly minimal, carry profound weight. What elevates them beyond mere physical actions is the deliberate simplicity married to unwavering focus. Every gesture matters because the healer has chosen it, understands it, believes in it.

Your own rituals should emerge from this same place of authentic connection. Start by identifying what already feels meaningful to you. Does the act of speaking aloud clarify your intention? Does touch—the physical stirring of a remedy or the holding of herbs between your palms—help you focus spiritual energy? Some healers find power in stillness and silent meditation, while others need movement, sound, even song.

The structure itself matters less than the consistency of practice and the depth of belief you bring to it.

When crafting a ritual for a specific remedy, begin by holding the primary ingredient and asking yourself what this plant needs to become medicine. Not just physical medicine, but *soul medicine*. What words, what prayers, what gestures honor both the plant's spirit and your healing intention? You might draw on traditional Appalachian prayers, invoke ancestral wisdom, or speak directly from your heart in your own words. The common thread is that your faith must infuse every syllable, every motion, every moment of preparation.

This is how ritual becomes a bridge between healer and remedy, transforming simple ingredients into vessels of profound healing power.

Faith as the Anchor of Intention

Faith doesn't float above your healing work like distant poetry. It anchors every step, transforming plant preparations into genuine medicine through the force of your conviction. Without this spiritual grounding, you're left with leaves in water—nothing more.

Begin with physical preparation as spiritual preparation. Clear your workspace deliberately, removing objects that scatter your attention. Wash your hands with slow awareness, feeling the water purify more than skin. Light a candle if fire focuses your mind. These opening gestures aren't theater; they're boundary markers separating ordinary time from sacred work. Your subconscious recognizes the shift, settling into the deeper awareness where healing power lives.

Hold the plant material in both palms. Notice its weight, texture, temperature. This tactile connection initiates relationship between your spirit and the plant's essence. Now speak your intention aloud in your own language, not borrowed formulas. "This elderberry tincture becomes medicine for persistent cough. I ask it to soothe inflamed tissue, clear congestion, restore easy breathing." Precision matters here. Vague prayers drift into vague results.

During physical preparation—steeping, grinding, mixing, binding —maintain rhythmic awareness of each movement. Stir clockwise to draw healing inward, counterclockwise to expel illness outward, keeping your mind locked on the outcome you're crafting (Koziol, 2020). Some healers count repetitions, using numbers that carry personal meaning. Others hum or pray continuously, letting sound carry focused energy into the remedy.

The moment before sealing the remedy holds particular power.

This is when doubt intrudes most strongly, whispering that you're merely mixing plants in water, that nothing extraordinary is happening. This is precisely when faith must assert itself most forcefully. Place both hands over your completed preparation and visualize—with absolute conviction—the healing already accomplished. See the person well, fever broken, pain dissolved. Hold this vision until it feels more solid than the doubt trying to undermine it.

Seal your work with declarative certainty. Not hope, not wish, but statement of fact: "This medicine carries healing. So it is." The conviction in those words completes the energetic circuit you've constructed throughout the ritual, locking your intention into the remedy's vibrational structure where it can do its work.

Record your process in simple detail—ingredients used, words spoken, gestures performed, the quality of your focus during preparation. This documentation serves dual purposes: replicating successful approaches and revealing patterns in how your faith strengthens through practice. When delivering the remedy, provide clear usage instructions, but resist explaining every spiritual component. The recipient needs enough understanding to align their own belief with the medicine's purpose. Your faith has already completed the essential work.

* * *

Creating Remedies with Plant Wisdom and Spiritual Intent

Harnessing Plant Energies

Start by walking familiar land with a different quality of attention. You're not identifying plants—you're feeling for vibration, that subtle current each living being broadcasts. Traditional practitioners describe it as pressure against the palm, warmth in the chest, sudden knowing that pulls you three steps left toward jewelweed you hadn't consciously noticed.

Plants generate electromagnetic fields measurable by scientific instruments, with research highlighting their bioelectrical signals for communication and growth (Volkov, 2012). Humans possess the biological capacity to detect these frequencies, though modern life has dulled the sensitivity. This isn't mystical abstraction but a recoverable skill embedded in your very biology. (Volkov, 2012)

Practice this: Choose a single plant you already know. Approach it slowly, stopping when you first sense *something*—that indefinable shift in the air. Extend your dominant hand, palm facing the plant, about six inches away. Close your eyes.

Don't search for sensation; let it arrive.

Some people feel tingling, others temperature change, a few experience color behind closed eyelids. There's no correct response. You're calibrating your awareness to frequencies you've ignored for years. Repeat this practice with the same plant species for seven consecutive days, ideally at the same time. By the fourth day, most people notice the sensation strengthening, arriving faster. You're not developing new abilities but recovering dormant ones.

The seventh visit, speak aloud: "Show me your medicine." Then sit in silence for ten minutes. Insights arrive as sudden thoughts, physical sensations in your own body, or emotional shifts. One practitioner consistently felt tightness in her throat near mullein, later learning it specifically treats respiratory congestion (Turker & Gurel, 2005)., a use well-documented in traditional herbal medicine (Turker & Gurel, 2005).

Document everything in a dedicated journal. Not poetic impressions—concrete physical sensations, times, weather conditions, your emotional state beforehand. Patterns emerge that reveal how your unique system receives information. When you've established relationship with three plants through this seven-day process, begin the identification work traditional healers practiced: matching plant vibration to human need.

Hold your non-dominant hand over a plant while placing your dominant hand on different body areas—forehead, throat, heart, stomach. Notice where the vibration intensifies. Yarrow might pulse strongest when your hand rests over a wound, reflecting its traditional use in healing (Ghorbani et al., 2017). Mint's energy might sharpen near your temples, aligning with its known efficacy for headache relief (Borhani Haghighi et al., 2010). This is vibrational correspondence—the plant showing you where its medicine concentrates. (Ghorbani et al., 2017)

Harvest only after this relationship exists. The chemical constituents remain identical whether you gather with reverence or indifference, but the energetic imprint differs entirely.

Infusing Remedies with Intention

When you prepare a healing remedy, the moment of intention-setting transforms simple herbs into vessels of profound spiritual power. This alchemy begins not with the grinding of roots or the steeping of leaves, but with the quiet centering of your own spirit. Before your hands touch a single plant, pause. Take three deliberate breaths, each one drawing you deeper into awareness of the sacred work ahead.

Setting your intention is a practice of spiritual focus. You're not simply deciding what you want the remedy to do—you're opening a channel between your faith, the plant's inherent wisdom, and the divine forces that animate all healing. Place your hands over the herbs you've gathered and speak your intention aloud, even if only in a whisper. Name the affliction you seek to address, but more importantly, name the wellness you wish to invoke. "I call forth this plant's power to ease pain and restore strength" carries far more spiritual weight than a vague hope for improvement.

The words themselves become part of the remedy's essence.

Many Appalachian healers incorporate prayer into this process, weaving Christian scripture with their knowledge of plant medicine. You might read Psalm 23 over a salve meant for protection, or recite words from the Gospel of John as you prepare a tea for healing. These sacred texts aren't mere accompaniment—they're active ingredients, infusing the remedy with layers of spiritual authority that your faith recognizes and amplifies. If your spiritual practice draws from different traditions, honor that. The key is *authenticity* in your belief, not adherence to any single form.

As you blend your ingredients, maintain focus on your intention. Stir clockwise while visualizing light flowing from your heart, through your hands, and into the mixture. Some practitioners sing old hymns or mountain songs during this process, their voices carrying intention into the remedy through sound and vibration. Others work in meditative silence, letting their concentrated faith do the speaking. Both approaches honor the sacred nature of the work.

The final step seals your spiritual intention into the physical remedy. Hold the completed preparation between your palms and offer it to the divine—however you understand that presence. Thank the plants for their sacrifice, acknowledge the ancestors whose wisdom guides your hands, and affirm your faith that this remedy will serve its intended purpose. This act of gratitude and affirmation completes the circuit of power, ensuring that when the remedy is used, it carries the full force of your faith-infused intention into the body and spirit of the one who receives it.

Blending Tradition with Innovation

This practice of blending intention with plant wisdom forms what earlier generations called the double medicine—where physical constituents and spiritual conviction work as inseparable partners. When you hold yarrow root in one palm and faith in the other, you're not choosing between them. You're recognizing that both operate through different laws, yet converge in the body of the person who receives your remedy.

Traditional Appalachian healers understood something modern herbalism often misses: the most potent remedies emerge when you honor established knowledge while remaining open to what the spirits reveal in your own time. A grandmother's salve recipe passed down through five generations carries accumulated power, yes. But that same grandmother likely adjusted proportions based on what the plants told her each season, what her prayers revealed about a specific person's need, what her dreams showed her the night before preparing medicine for a particularly stubborn ailment. This blend of empirical observation, inherited wisdom, and intuitive spiritual guidance is characteristic of Appalachian folk medicine.

This isn't abandoning tradition for novelty. It's recognizing that *living traditions breathe.*

Consider how elder healers approached seasonal variations. When drought stressed the mullein, making leaves smaller and more concentrated, they didn't simply follow old measurements. They held those stressed leaves and listened—sometimes reducing the amount used, other times recognizing that hardship had intensified the plant's medicine in ways that demanded different preparation methods entirely. They trusted both the inherited wisdom and their own developed sensitivity to plant communication. That dual trust produced remedies perfectly calibrated to circumstance.

You can cultivate this same responsiveness without disrespecting lineage. Start with traditional formulas exactly as taught, preparing them multiple times until the process becomes second nature. Then, as you work, pay attention to subtle deviations that arise not from carelessness but from genuine intuitive prompting. Maybe you feel called to add three drops of tincture instead of five. Maybe the stirring rhythm wants to slow despite what you've been taught. These impulses deserve investigation, not immediate acceptance or reflexive dismissal.

Test variations methodically. Prepare one batch using the traditional method and another incorporating your intuited adjustment, keeping detailed records of both. Note not just physical results but the quality of healing—how quickly relief comes, how thoroughly it penetrates, whether it addresses root causes or merely symptoms. Over time, you'll distinguish between random impulse and genuine spiritual guidance.

The path forward requires you to become both faithful student and discerning innovator, holding reverence for what the ancestors preserved while trusting that the same spirits who taught them still speak. Your hands carry forward their wisdom. Your faith activates the same forces they commanded. The plants growing outside your door contain the same essential medicines, though the world around them has shifted dramatically.

What comes next builds on everything you've learned about protection, intention, and plant collaboration, turning toward the specific challenge of ancestral connection—where the dead themselves become your most powerful allies in healing work that spans generations.

CHAPTER 7

Secret 6: Establishing A Rooted Personal Practice Aligned With Mountain Wisdom

---

Creating Sacred Spaces: The Art of Altar Work

Foundations of Altar Creation

In many historical households, particularly across various folk traditions, specific domestic spaces served as focal points for spiritual attention and intention. For example, in 19th-century American homes, the mantelpiece or a dedicated shelf often held cherished objects: a family Bible, photographs of ancestors, sentimental mementos, or items gathered from significant places. These weren't merely decorative arrangements; they functioned as operational spiritual anchors, physical points where intention concentrated and personal or familial devotions could be directed with precision.

An altar is never about the objects themselves.

It exists as the point where your spiritual attention returns daily, building power through repetition the way water carves stone through persistent contact rather than force. This return, this consistent acknowledgment, transforms an ordinary surface into something consecrated. The power doesn't reside in the candle or the photograph or the stone you carried back from the mountain. The power accumulates in the act of coming back, day after day, with focused awareness and spiritual intent.

The foundational element is intention—not vague spiritual aspiration, but clear, directed purpose. Before a single object finds its place, you must know what you're building and why. Are you creating a space for ancestral communion? For protection work? For daily devotion to the divine? For strengthening your connection to the land spirits? Your altar's purpose shapes every choice that follows, from placement to arrangement to the objects you invite into that sacred geography.

Personal symbolism follows naturally from this clarity. The objects you choose should resonate with your own spiritual understanding, not borrowed aesthetics or someone else's tradition. A worn river stone might hold more power for you than the most expensive crystal if that stone came from a place of personal significance, gathered with reverence and intention. Your grandmother's thimble, a sprig of cedar from the mountain behind your home, a faded photograph—these carry authentic spiritual weight because they're woven into the fabric of your own story and faith.

Symbolism and Sacred Objects

Choosing objects for your altar is an act of spiritual translation—taking the invisible currents of faith, memory, and intention and anchoring them in the tangible world. These aren't decorations. They're the physical vocabulary of your practice, each piece a word in an ongoing conversation with the divine and the land.

Every object you place becomes a vessel. A stone from a mountain stream doesn't merely sit there—it carries the memory of water, the coolness of shade, the persistence of ancient rock. A white candle holds more than flame; it embodies purity, the clarity of focused intention, or the presence of ancestral light depending on what you ask it to bear. The meaning doesn't reside in the object itself but in the relationship you forge with it through reverence and use.

Consider how your grandmother's photograph becomes more than an image. It's a doorway, a point of contact with lineage and wisdom that stretches back beyond memory. A bundle of dried herbs gathered with gratitude transforms into protection, healing, or blessing. The bowl of water you place at the altar's edge shifts from simple liquid to something liminal—a mirror, a boundary between worlds, a symbol of emotional depth and spiritual cleansing.

You are the one who assigns this sacred meaning, not through wishful thinking but through deliberate choice and sustained devotion. When you light that candle with clear intention, when you speak to that photograph as though your ancestors truly listen—because they do—you activate the spiritual architecture you've built. Your altar becomes a living threshold where the material and the mystical meet, shaped entirely by your faith and the attention you bring to it.

Rituals and Daily Practices

Most altars die from neglect disguised as completion. You build them with care, arrange each object thoughtfully, light the candle with conviction—and then they become static shrines gathering dust while your spiritual life happens elsewhere.

An altar only lives when it receives your presence. Daily engagement transforms arranged objects into active spiritual technology. This doesn't require elaborate ritual. Sometimes it's thirty seconds of intentional acknowledgment: lighting a candle, speaking gratitude aloud, touching the stone you brought from the creek while remembering why it matters. What counts is consistency, the deliberate return that signals to both spirits and your own consciousness that this space remains sacred and attended.

The rhythm builds spiritual momentum. When you show up each morning to refresh water, adjust a photograph, or simply stand before your altar speaking your intentions, you're not performing ceremony—you're maintaining relationship. The ancestors learn to expect you. The land spirits recognize your devotion. Your own faith deepens through the accumulated weight of small acts repeated until they become as natural as breathing.

Yet living altars must also evolve. The objects that called to you six months ago may no longer resonate with your current spiritual needs. *This is not failure.* A father's pocketknife might replace a grandmother's brooch as you seek different ancestral guidance. Protective herbs gathered in autumn give way to spring flowers representing renewal. The Bible you've used for years might shift position, making room for a bowl of graveyard dirt as you deepen into ancestor work. Pay attention when objects lose their charge or new items insist on inclusion—your altar speaks through these impulses, revealing how your practice is shifting beneath conscious awareness.

Seasonal changes demand recognition too.

The altar that served you through winter's introspection requires different energy as spring arrives with its insistence on growth and action. This isn't arbitrary redecorating but spiritual responsiveness, aligning your practice with the land's rhythms and your own transformation. Remove what has completed its purpose with gratitude. Welcome what arrives next with intention.

The altar you tend daily for months develops presence you can feel when you enter the room—a thickness in the air, a gravitational pull toward the space. This accumulation of focused attention and spiritual exchange creates exactly what mountain practitioners understood: sacred space isn't built once but cultivated continuously through devoted care.

* * *

Honoring the Seasons: Celebrating Appalachian and Christian Traditions

The Rhythms of Nature

Mountain seasons pulse with spiritual energy that transforms both landscape and practice. When you attune yourself to these rhythms, you discover that the Appalachian year creates its own calendar of power, marking times when particular spiritual work becomes amplified or when the veil between worlds grows thin enough to touch.

Spring arrives late in high elevations, often not settling until late April, bringing a surge of raw creative force (The Wilderness Society, n.d.). The land explodes with growth after months of dormancy, and this concentrated vitality flows into every plant pushing through soil. Practitioners who gather spring greens like ramps and watercress during this window work with medicine at its most potent, charged with the season's aggressive life force. This energy extends beyond wildcrafting—

spring serves prosperity work and fresh starts, when intentions planted mirror seeds breaking winter ground.

Summer in the mountains carries a different quality than lowland heat. The long, warm days create ideal conditions for protection work and spiritual fortification, when the sun's strength can be channeled into charms and wards. This is when elderflowers bloom and St. John's wort reaches peak potency, both traditional allies in shielding work. The abundance of the season supports gratitude rituals and offerings to land spirits, acknowledging the generosity flowing from soil and sky.

Autumn transforms the mountains into a landscape of endings and preparation. As leaves turn and fall, the energy shifts inward, making this the season for *ancestral work and divination*. The thinning veil at Samhain has deep roots here, where mountain people have long honored their dead during harvest time. This is when you gather the final herbs, preserve medicines for winter, and turn your practice toward reflection and communion with those who walked these ridges before you.

Winter demands a different kind of attention—a season of stillness that teaches the power of rest and dream work.

Integrating Christian and Mountain Rituals

Many Appalachian households, especially in the mid-20th century, followed a "doubled calendar." They observed Christmas on December twenty-fifth with church services and nativity scenes, but also on January sixth for Old Christmas, when some left bread and salt for wandering spirits. Easter often included both sunrise service at the local church and a predawn walk to gather dew from specific plants, bottled for healing work throughout the year.

This wasn't confusion; it was spiritual completeness.

The region's isolation allowed Christianity and folk practice to fuse rather than conflict, creating a spiritual vocabulary where both traditions spoke to different chambers of the same heart. Your grandmother might quote scripture over her healing herbs while simultaneously acknowledging the land spirits that made those herbs potent. She saw no contradiction because there was none—each practice strengthened the other, woven together like the threads of a charm bag.

When you honor this duality in your own practice, you're not picking sides. You're recognizing that sacred time operates on multiple frequencies. The Christian calendar marks one rhythm; the turning wheel of the seasons marks another. Both deserve reverence. Both hold power.

Start by observing which holidays already resonate with you, whether that's the solemnity of Good Friday or the wild joy of May Day. Then explore their counterparts in the other tradition. Notice where they overlap, where they diverge, and where they create something entirely new when held together. This is how mountain wisdom works —not through rigid categories, but through the patient art of holding space for mystery.

Crafting Seasonal Celebrations

Creating a seasonal celebration begins with choosing one moment in the year that calls to you—not what you think should matter, but what actually pulls at your attention. Maybe it's the first hard frost, or the week when dogwoods bloom, or the particular quality of October light.

Once you've identified your moment, spend time observing it without agenda. Go outside. Notice what's happening in the natural world: which plants are dying back, which animals are active, how the air smells, where shadows fall. This direct observation becomes the foundation of authentic ritual.

Next, consider what this seasonal shift means for your life practically and spiritually. Spring planting isn't just agricultural—it's about what you're beginning internally. Autumn harvest isn't only about gathering crops; it's about recognizing what efforts have matured and what needs releasing. Your celebration should acknowledge both the land's rhythm and your own parallel transformation.

Now build your ritual from three simple elements: something you say, something you do, and something you offer. The words might be a prayer, a psalm, or your own statement of gratitude and intention. The action could be lighting a candle at dawn, walking a specific path, or burying something symbolic. The offering establishes reciprocity—cornmeal to the land, whiskey poured at a threshold, bread left for birds.

Avoid complexity.

A seasonal celebration that requires an hour of preparation and exotic materials won't survive past the first year. The power accumulates through repetition across years, not through elaborate one-time performances. Consider how traditional practices already embedded in your life might serve as starting points. If your family always planted by the signs, that's a framework. If you attend Easter sunrise service, you can add a predawn walk to gather dew. If Halloween feels significant, explore its connections to ancestral communion and the thinning veil between worlds.

Document your celebration in writing—not for social media, but for yourself next year when details blur. Note what you said, what you noticed, how you felt. This creates continuity.

Over time, your personal celebrations will develop weight and presence. You'll feel the approach of your chosen day differently. The ritual actions will carry accumulated meaning. This is how folk practice actually works—not through perfection, but through devoted return to what matters.

* * *

Prayer and Ritual: Weaving Daily Practices with Mountain Wisdom

The Art of Daily Prayer

Prayer in Appalachian practice happens at the stove while stirring soup, at the fence line feeding chickens, at the bedside before sleep—not only at formal occasions. This deep integration of spirituality into daily life is a hallmark of folk traditions. You're building relationship through repetition, not performing ritual for singular effect.

Start with morning prayer before your feet touch the floor. Speak aloud if possible—voice carries power that silent thought cannot match. A simple structure: gratitude first, then protection, then intention. "Thank you for this day and breath in my body. Keep harm from my threshold and those I love. Guide my hands to right work." Fifteen seconds. The words matter less than the daily return to them.

Kitchen prayers transform cooking into medicine. As you prepare food, speak blessing over it. "May this nourish and heal. May it carry strength to those who eat it." Coffee made with prayer becomes different than coffee made distracted. Water blessed before drinking becomes deliberate hydration rather than mechanical consumption. These aren't elaborate invocations—they're conscious acknowledgment that everything you handle can carry intention or remain inert.

Threshold prayers create energetic boundaries most practitioners ignore until trouble arrives. Before leaving home, touch the doorframe and speak protection over the space you're leaving and the path ahead. "This house stands in safety. This journey unfolds in grace. I return whole." Before entering home again, pause at the door to leave the day's chaos outside. These transitions mark spiritual shifts, not just physical ones. Doorways are liminal spaces where energy concentrates—use them deliberately.

Evening prayer closes the day's circuit. Review what happened without judgment, release what you cannot change, acknowledge what you're carrying into sleep. "I release what isn't mine. I keep what serves. I rest in protection." This isn't psychotherapy—it's energetic hygiene, clearing accumulated static before unconsciousness makes you vulnerable.

The pattern matters more than perfection. Miss a day without guilt, return the next morning without drama. You're training spiritual muscle through consistent small effort, not achieving enlightenment through intensity. After thirty days, these prayers become automatic anchors. After ninety, they restructure how you move through the world. After a year, you'll notice their absence immediately when disrupted.

That's when you know the practice has taken root.

Rituals of the Natural Cycle

Building seasonal practice doesn't require elaborate ceremony—it requires noticing and returning. Choose four moments in the year that carry genuine weight for you, then construct simple rituals you can sustain across decades.

Spring equinox marks the moment when light overtakes darkness. On that morning, or within three days either side, clear your threshold. Sweep the front steps physically, then sweep them again with intention while speaking aloud: "Winter leaves, growth enters. What was stuck now moves." Burn dried sage or rosemary at the doorway. Plant something—even a single seed in a cup of dirt. The act matters more than the outcome.

Summer solstice celebrates peak power and protection. Gather at dawn if you can manage it. Collect dew from plants with your bare hands, touching your face and throat with the moisture while speaking gratitude for health and safety. If you keep a garden, walk its perimeter with salt water, marking boundaries. If you don't, walk your property line or your apartment threshold. Light a candle at noon and let it burn completely, speaking protection over your household as it burns.

Autumn equinox opens the door to ancestors.

Set a plate at your table with portions of your meal and speak to those who've passed. Name them if you knew them, or simply say "those who came before me" if lineage is broken or unknown. Leave the plate until morning, then return the food to earth. This isn't symbolic—you're feeding relationship across the veil. Notice what dreams arrive in the following week.

Winter solstice demands stillness. The longest night belongs to rest and dreaming. Extinguish all electric light for one hour after sunset. Sit in darkness without distraction, listening to silence. Speak aloud what you're releasing from the passing year. Write it on paper if that helps, then burn the paper safely. Before sleep, ask for guidance through dreams. Keep water and paper beside your bed to record what arrives before it dissolves.

These four anchors create a rhythmic container for everything else. Mark them on your calendar now. Prepare one day ahead so you're not scrambling. Repeat them exactly for three years before changing anything—*consistency builds power* that innovation cannot.

Blending Christian and Folk Traditions

Appalachian folk magic resists the false division between sacred and secular, between Christian prayer and the old ways. The same woman who taught children their catechism knew precisely which tree to petition for fever bark, and she saw no contradiction (Blue Ridge Tales, 2025). (Milnes, 2025). (Kimball, 2025). in either act. Both were expressions of a singular truth: the divine moves through all things, and we address it through whatever language opens the channel most clearly.

This blending creates friction for many modern practitioners. You might recite Psalm 91 for protection but feel self-conscious speaking directly to plants. You leave offerings for land spirits yet worry it contradicts your Christian upbringing. *This internal conflict poisons the work before it begins.*

The path forward isn't choosing one tradition over another—it's honoring both with equal sincerity. When you light a candle and speak a prayer, you're not performing separate acts of Christian devotion and folk magic. You're engaging a unified spiritual reality that responds to genuine faith, regardless of which cultural vocabulary you employ. The Bible itself speaks of trees clapping their hands and stones crying out; creation has always been alive with spirit.

Begin where your belief feels most natural. If scripture grounds you, start your daily practice with a passage that resonates—perhaps Psalm 121 for protection or Proverbs for wisdom. Follow this with a simple acknowledgment of the land spirits where you live, speaking as you would to respected neighbors. Your offerings need not be elaborate: spring water, a pinch of cornmeal, honest words of gratitude.

As your practice deepens, the boundary between traditions will blur naturally. You'll find yourself weaving biblical verses into plant-gathering prayers without conscious thought. Your ancestor altar might hold both a cross and a bowl of herbs gathered under the waning moon. This isn't contradiction—it's wholeness.

The litmus test is simple: does the practice strengthen your connection to the sacred, or does it create distance through doubt? Choose the elements that genuinely resonate, then practice them without apology. Your uncertainty matters less than your consistency. Faith grows through accumulated evidence, not intellectual resolution.

Crafting Personal Rituals

Crafting your own rituals is where the true heart of Appalachian folk magic comes alive in your hands. The old ways are meant to be held, shaped, and worn smooth by your own touch—not simply memorized like lines in a play. When you create rituals that speak to your unique beliefs and spiritual connections, you're not straying from the tradition; you're keeping it breathing.

Start small, with something that already carries meaning for you.

Maybe it's the way you greet the morning sun through the kitchen window, or how you stir your coffee counterclockwise to banish worry before the day begins. These simple acts become sacred when you recognize them as such. The ritual doesn't need candles, incantations, or elaborate preparation—though it certainly can have them. What it needs is your *intention* and your willingness to show up with reverence, day after day.

Consider the rhythm of your life and where the sacred already tries to enter. Do you walk the same path each evening? Does the scent of particular herbs make you feel rooted and safe? Notice these threads and weave them deliberately into your practice. You might craft a ritual for stirring protection into your home by sweeping the threshold with intention each morning, or honor the land spirits by leaving water for them beneath the old oak in your yard. The most powerful rituals are those that feel like homecoming, not performance.

Remember that personal rituals grow and change just as you do. What serves you in one season may need adjustment in another. This isn't failure—it's faithfulness to the living nature of the practice. Trust your instincts, listen to the quiet voice that whispers what feels right, and honor the ancestral wisdom that flows through your blood. Your rituals should reflect who you are *and* where you come from, bridging the personal with the traditional in a way that feeds your spirit and strengthens your connection to the mountain wisdom that endures.

CHAPTER 8

Living The Secrets: Integration, Integrity, And The Ongoing Path Of Faith-Rooted Practice

—✦—

Integrating the Secrets into Daily Life

Weaving Practices into Routine

A woman I knew kept a Mason jar of salt and rainwater on her kitchen windowsill for thirty years. She added three drops to her dishwater every morning, not because her grandmother told her to—though she had—but because the act itself became a threshold between sleep and waking, between ordinary and sacred. When she washed her family's breakfast plates, she wasn't just cleaning. She was renewing protection, clearing accumulated tension, preparing vessels that would nourish bodies already blessed by her intention.

This is what integration actually looks like.

Daily practice doesn't require dedicated ritual space or uninterrupted hours. It requires recognizing that every repeated action creates spiritual architecture. The coffee you brew can become an act of gratitude if you pause long enough to speak thanks—to the water, to the mountain soil that grew the beans, to the hands that harvested them. The threshold you cross leaving home can become a protective boundary if you touch the doorframe with intention, visualizing a shield that travels with you. These aren't additions to your routine. They're transformations of what already exists.

Most people fail at integration because they're waiting for the right conditions. They believe morning devotions require candlelight and silence, that protection work demands elaborate preparation. But my grandmother worked her strongest magic while shelling peas, her lips moving in almost-silent prayer as her hands moved through repetitive motion. The rhythm itself became trance. The peas became offerings. The bowl became altar.

Evening reflection operates similarly. You don't need journaling prompts or structured meditation. What you need is the discipline to pause before sleep and ask: "What crossed my threshold today?" Not metaphorically—literally. Who entered your home? What energies did they carry? What did you bring back from the grocery store, the workplace, the argument you had in traffic? This simple inventory allows you to identify what requires clearing before you carry it into vulnerable sleep.

One practice I recommend without reservation: keep a small dish of salt near where you remove your shoes. Touch it when you come home. Let that tactile moment become a reminder that you're crossing back into protected space, that the day's accumulation doesn't follow you further. Some practitioners whisper a specific phrase. Others simply exhale deliberately. The consistency matters more than the elaboration.

Ancestral wisdom integrates most powerfully through inherited gestures. If your grandmother knocked on wood, you're already carrying protective magic in your muscle memory. If your father threw spilled salt over his shoulder, you inherited an understanding that certain substances require specific responses. These aren't superstitions to overcome. They're doorways into deeper practice, waiting for you to recognize what you've been doing all along.

Maintaining Authenticity and Respect

Authenticity means knowing what you're actually doing, not just performing borrowed motions. When you speak a charm, you should understand the tradition that shaped those words—not academically, but spiritually. You should know whether you're invoking Cherokee plant wisdom, Scottish threshold protection, or Christian folk benediction, and more importantly, whether you have genuine relationship with any of those streams.

This matters because Appalachian folk magic isn't a buffet.

Cultural appropriation happens when people extract techniques from their spiritual context, treating living traditions like decorative elements. A white practitioner burning sage while calling on spirits they've never honored, in a tradition they've never studied, using land they've never listened to—that's theft dressed as spirituality. But the question gets more complex in Appalachian practice specifically, because this tradition already represents synthesis. It emerged from genuine necessity when different peoples shared actual geography, actual hardship, actual spiritual exchange over generations.

The difference lies in *relationship and lineage.*

If your family comes from these mountains, you're already embedded in the spiritual architecture even if you're learning practices your immediate ancestors forgot. If you have Cherokee ancestry, certain plant relationships belong to you by inheritance. If you carry African diasporic lineage, particular spirit work connects to your blood. But if you're approaching from outside these streams entirely, you need to ask harder questions.

Respect requires three non-negotiable commitments. First, learn the actual history—not romanticized versions, but the genuine circumstances that created these practices, including displacement, enslavement, and cultural survival under pressure. Second, acknowledge your sources explicitly. If you're adapting Cherokee herbalism, say so. If you're drawing from Hoodoo techniques that entered mountain practice through African American rootworkers, name that debt. Third, never teach what you haven't lived long enough to understand in your body.

I've watched people collect practices like trophies, assembling altars with items from six different traditions they encountered last month. That's not synthesis. Synthesis happens slowly, over lifetimes, when traditions meet through sustained contact and genuine need. What you can do instead is commit deeply to one stream and allow it to teach you properly before reaching for another.

The test is simple: Can you explain *why* you're doing what you're doing?

Not just the technique, but the spiritual logic underneath it? Can you name who taught you, directly or through lineage? Can you articulate what you're giving back to the tradition, the land, the community that holds this knowledge? If those questions create defensiveness rather than clarity, you're probably reaching for something that isn't yours yet.

Integrity means practicing only what you've genuinely earned through relationship, study, and time. Everything else is performance.

Personal Transformation Through Practice

Real transformation doesn't announce itself with thunder. You don't wake up one morning suddenly enlightened because you burned the right candle or spoke the right charm. What happens instead is quieter and more permanent: you notice one day that you've stopped asking permission from your own doubt.

The shift happens in accumulated moments.

After months of daily altar work, you reach for your grandmother's photograph without thinking, the gesture as automatic as breathing. You find yourself noticing which plants grow where, tracking moon phases without consulting calendars, speaking protective words over your threshold because the practice has become who you are rather than what you do. These aren't dramatic revelations—they're the evidence that something fundamental has changed in how you inhabit the world. Personal growth through folk magic practice looks different than what self-help culture promises.

You don't become a better version of yourself through positive thinking. You become more *coherent*. The scattered parts of your identity—inherited faith, ancestral memory, relationship with land, daily choices—start aligning into something with actual structural integrity. When you speak a charm with conviction, you're speaking from that unified place rather than hoping words will compensate for internal fragmentation.

Spiritual connection deepens because you've built the infrastructure for it.

Ancestors who seemed distant or silent begin appearing in dreams because you've created consistent space for them at your altar, offered them attention and tobacco and honest conversation for long enough that the relationship has become mutual. Land spirits respond because you've proven you're not extracting—you're participating. The Cherokee concept of *duyvkta*, of being in right relationship with all things, stops being philosophy and becomes lived experience (Conley, 2007). (Riggs, 2018). This empowerment isn't about control.

It's about knowing exactly where you stand in the invisible architecture of the world. You understand which protections you've built and how they function. You know which plants have taught you their uses through direct relationship rather than books. You can trace the logic of your practices back through generations, understanding not just the techniques but the survival necessity that forged them. That knowledge creates a kind of spiritual confidence that can't be faked or purchased—it only emerges through sustained practice that's tested itself against actual circumstance.

Faith shifts from belief to experience. You're no longer hoping your protective work functions; you've watched it function repeatedly. You're no longer borrowing someone else's cosmology; you've built your own through direct contact with the forces that cosmology describes. The sacred words you speak carry power because you've discovered personally that certain words become doorways when spoken with absolute conviction, not because an authority told you to recite them.

The cost is you can't go back to passive spiritual consumption. Once you've lived this way long enough, surface practices feel hollow. You've tasted what genuine relationship with the unseen world requires, and anything less becomes obviously insufficient.

* * *

Navigating Cultural Sensitivity and Tradition

Respecting Appalachian Traditions

Cultural respect begins with recognizing that Appalachian folk magic isn't neutral territory available for anyone to harvest. This tradition carries blood memory—the accumulated knowledge of people who survived through these practices when no doctor would come to the hollow, when the law offered no protection, when community meant the difference between winter starvation and survival. Families paid for this knowledge with their dead: children who didn't survive before the right fever cure was discovered, women who died in childbirth before the midwife learned which plants could stop hemorrhage. That cost matters.

When you approach these practices, you're approaching something people died to preserve.

The difference between *respectful engagement* and appropriation isn't about bloodline. My own lineage traces back to these mountains, but I've watched people with no mountain connection practice this work with profound reverence, and I've seen those born here treat it like theater. Ancestry grants you nothing automatically—it only means you carry different responsibilities. What determines respect is how you answer three questions: Do you understand what you're actually doing? Can you name who taught you and what tradition they're carrying? And critically—are you giving anything back?

That third question trips people up.

Reciprocity in cultural practice doesn't mean paying for knowledge. It means tending the tradition itself: learning the actual history, including the uncomfortable parts. Acknowledging explicitly that this synthesis emerged from Scottish-Irish immigrants, Cherokee peoples, and African Americans sharing hardship and spiritual technology across generations of proximity and exchange. Speaking those origins aloud instead of vaguely gesturing toward "mountain wisdom." Teaching only what you've lived long enough to understand in your bones, not what you read last month. Supporting the communities this knowledge comes from, not just extracting their wisdom for your personal practice.

Authenticity requires time. You cannot speed-run genuine relationship with a living tradition.

The practice itself will teach you this—your first attempts at spirit communication will feel awkward and performative because they are. Your protective workings won't hold power initially because faith develops through accumulated evidence, not borrowed confidence. This isn't failure; it's the tradition sorting sincere practitioners from spiritual tourists. The ones who stay are the ones willing to feel foolish while learning, to repeat simple practices for months before results appear, to accept that mastery arrives in years rather than weekends.

Watch for the moment when you stop performing the tradition and start being changed by it. That's when awkward altar-tending becomes actual ancestral communion. When copied protection work becomes something you'd stake your safety on. When you realize you're no longer practicing Appalachian folk magic—you're living inside a worldview where every threshold holds spiritual significance and reciprocity governs all exchange. That transformation only happens through sustained, humble attention to practices whose logic you're still learning to inhabit.

Understanding Cultural Appropriation

Consider the widespread commercialization of smudging, a sacred purification ritual practiced by various Indigenous North American peoples for millennia. Within the modern wellness industry, influencers and brands frequently promote "smudge kits" with white sage, demonstrating its use for "clearing negative energy." These presentations often detach the practice from its profound spiritual and cultural roots, simplifying it into a performative aesthetic or consumer product.

What is frequently omitted is the intricate ceremonial significance and deep lineage of smudging. For many Indigenous communities, smudging is a vital act of spiritual cleansing, prayer, and connection, utilizing specific sacred plants like white sage or cedar according to precise traditions passed down through generations. These practices are integral to cultural identity and well-being, not merely a trend for superficial "wellness" benefits.

Real harm has occurred. The surge in demand fueled by commercialization has led to the overharvesting of sacred plants like white sage, pushing them towards endangerment and limiting access for Indigenous communities who rely on them for traditional ceremonies. Sacred rituals that sustained cultures are reduced to "trendy folk spells" in lifestyle blogs and sold as commodities, contributing to cultural erosion. Genuine practitioners face requests for simplified, performative versions rather than an understanding of the profound stewardship and spiritual commitment these practices truly entail. This illustrates the mechanics of appropriation: extraction without relationship, teaching without lineage, profit without reciprocity.

When the original practitioners tried explaining the historical context—that smudging meant something entirely different when performed within its sacred framework—they were told they were "gatekeeping" and that "all knowledge wants to be free." But knowledge isn't neutral data. These practices encode survival strategies, spiritual technologies tested across generations of crisis, and the accumulated faith of people who had no other options.

The test for responsible engagement is discomfortingly simple: *wait*. If you've been studying this tradition for less than three years, you're not ready to teach it. If you can't name specific people who taught you and describe their connection to the tradition, you don't have permission to share it publicly. If you're making money from these practices while the communities that preserved them still face poverty and marginalization, you're extracting rather than participating.

Consent in traditional knowledge doesn't work like consent for published information. Just because you found something in a book doesn't mean you have the right to teach it. The question isn't "can I legally do this?" but "should I?" Ask yourself: Who benefits from my sharing this? Am I contributing to understanding or to dilution? Would the people who died protecting this knowledge recognize what I'm doing as honorable?

Maintaining Authenticity and Integrity

Authenticity in Appalachian folk magic isn't about collecting the right objects or reciting the perfect words. It begins with an uncomfortable reckoning with yourself, a moment where you must answer truthfully: *What am I truly doing here, and why does it matter to me?* Not the version you'd share with others, not the romanticized vision of yourself as a practitioner—the raw, unvarnished truth. Write it down. If your answer feels vague, if it drifts toward "connecting with ancient wisdom" or "seeking powerful energy," you haven't reached honesty yet.

Document your sources with the care of a lineage keeper. Not for academic rigor, but for spiritual integrity. In a physical notebook—something tangible that holds weight—record every book, every teacher, every practice you've adopted, and note precisely how you came to learn it. When you cannot trace a practice back to a legitimate, respectful source, you've discovered the edge of authentic work. That boundary is sacred.

Now turn to your altar.

Pick up each object resting there and ask it why it belongs. If the answer is "it looked atmospheric" or "I saw someone use it online," set it aside. An altar isn't décor or performance art. It's a functional space of spiritual communion built from genuine relationship. Your grandmother's worn Bible belongs if you're truly honoring ancestral faith and she taught you to pray over its pages. A decorative vintage bottle purchased because it "felt witchy" does not, no matter how you've justified it. The objects that remain after this honest accounting form the foundation of your authentic practice.

Create a daily accountability ritual that demands truth. Before any magical work, speak aloud: "I'm doing this because..." and "I learned this from..." If you hesitate, if your voice catches or your heart resists, stop immediately. That discomfort is your integrity speaking, and it deserves your attention. Practice only what you can claim with certainty about its origins and your right to engage with it.

When you feel called to build new practices, begin with documented tradition rather than improvisation. If you're drawn to a protection charm, research its historical roots with genuine curiosity. What community practiced this? Under what circumstances? What materials did they actually use, and why? Adapt only after you understand the original spiritual logic so thoroughly you could explain it to someone without consulting your notes. This depth of understanding transforms borrowing into respectful engagement.

Notice who teaches you and what they require in return. Legitimate teachers don't package "secret mountain wisdom" into expensive weekend intensives. They share knowledge slowly, relationally, often expecting months of observation and participation before offering anything substantive. They correct misunderstandings without shame and set clear boundaries. If someone promises to reveal an entire tradition in forty-eight hours for the right price, you're purchasing performance, not inheriting practice.

Ground everything in personal faith cultivated through consistent devotion. Spend time daily—even just ten minutes—in prayer or meditation addressing the divine presence you genuinely believe in, not the one that sounds most mystical. This faith, honest and unadorned, becomes the coherent foundation that holds your entire practice together. Without it, you're simply rearranging symbols and hoping for magic.

* * *

Empowering Transformation Through Faith

The Alchemy of Faith

Faith isn't something you have. It's something you build, deliberately, through physical action repeated until the body knows what the mind still doubts. Mountain practitioners understood this instinctively—they didn't wait to feel certain before speaking healing words over a fevered child. They acted, and certainty followed.

Begin with the smallest possible commitment. Choose one practice you can perform daily in under two minutes. Not an elaborate ritual—something so simple refusal becomes harder than compliance. Light a candle each morning and speak three words of gratitude aloud before extinguishing it. That's the entire practice. No visualization, no elaborate intentions, no performance. Just flame, words, breath. Repeat this identically for thirty consecutive days without variation or expansion.

What you're actually doing is training your spiritual musculature through repetition, the same way a pianist develops finger independence through scales. The content matters less than the consistency. You're proving to yourself and to the spiritual forces observing that you show up. That reliability becomes the foundation everything else builds on.

After thirty days of identical repetition, add a second element: physical threshold acknowledgment. Each time you cross your home's entrance, touch the doorframe and speak a single sentence of protection. "This house stands under blessing." "Harm turns back at this boundary." The specific words matter less than the absolute conviction with which you speak them. You're not performing theater for invisible audiences—you're stating facts about reality with the same certainty you'd use to say "this door is wood."

Track observable results in a dedicated notebook, but not the way you expect. Don't record whether "magic worked." Instead, document concrete details: how the practice felt physically, what thoughts arose during it, any unusual occurrences within twenty-four hours afterward, however mundane. A neighbor's unexpected kindness. A stranger's smile. A bill arriving smaller than anticipated. You're training yourself to recognize communication from spiritual forces that rarely announces itself with thunder and lightning. Most divine response arrives through the small adjustments in daily reality that skepticism dismisses as coincidence.

Within three months of this minimal but absolute consistency, something shifts.

The practices stop feeling like something you're doing *to* reality and start feeling like participation *with* forces that were already reaching toward you, waiting for reliable contact. That shift—from performance to partnership—is where authentic power lives. Faith transforms from concept into tool only through this unglamorous repetition. The mountain tradition survived because practitioners couldn't afford spiritual tourism. They needed results, so they showed up daily until showing up became who they were.

Personal Narratives of Transformation

Real transformation rarely looks like the stories we tell ourselves about magic.

Anna, from a rural community in Appalachia, found herself turning to her grandmother's folk remedies during a period of profound uncertainty—not because she fully believed in their magical power, but because she felt she had exhausted all other practical avenues. Her grandmother's instructions for making a protective 'spirit water' seemed archaic: spring water collected at specific moon phases, specific herbs, and a whispered blessing. Anna felt a profound sense of skepticism the first morning she performed the ritual, standing in the predawn chill. Yet, with nothing left to lose, she persisted. After several weeks of consistent practice, she noticed a subtle shift: her chronic anxiety lessened, and she felt a newfound sense of calm wash over her in situations that once would have sent her spiraling. She hadn't expected healing—she'd barely allowed herself to hope for it. But the simple act of repeating the ritual, of honoring the tradition with intention, had opened something within her. The faith didn't arrive before the practice; it grew slowly, quietly, *through* the practice itself.

That's the secret most folks miss.

Then there was James, a man who'd grown up hearing his great-aunt's stories about protection charms but had dismissed them as superstition until a string of misfortunes left him desperate. He crafted a simple charm following her instructions—red thread, iron nails, and whispered prayers at his doorway. The first night, nothing happened. The second night, the same. But by the third week, he noticed that the oppressive feeling that had followed him for months began to lift.

His sleep improved. His luck seemed to turn. Was it the charm itself, or was it the faith he'd slowly begun to cultivate through the nightly ritual? He couldn't say for certain, and perhaps that was the point. The practice had given him something to believe in again, and that belief had become the foundation for genuine change.

These aren't tales of instant miracles or dramatic revelations. They're stories of people who showed up—day after day, ritual after ritual—and found that the mountain wisdom they'd inherited carried a deeper truth than they'd imagined. Faith doesn't always announce itself with thunder; sometimes it arrives as a whisper, growing stronger with each deliberate act of devotion.

Practical Steps for Deepening Faith

Mountain magic doesn't demand perfection—it demands presence. What matters isn't flawless ritual execution or encyclopedic plant knowledge, but the willingness to return each day with honest intention. You've encountered the seven secrets not as distant mystical concepts but as practical spiritual technologies: the synthesis of traditions that created something more potent than any single lineage, the relational foundation where spirits respond to consistency rather than commands, the recognition of plants as conscious allies rather than botanical resources. You've learned that protection works through layered collaboration between materials and intention, that healing requires the practitioner's complete internal alignment, and that faith itself becomes the bridge transforming ordinary action into genuine magic.

None of this activates through understanding alone.

The transformation happens in the repetition you'll undertake tomorrow morning, and the morning after that, and the one following. When you light that candle at your altar for the hundredth time, when your hands know the rhythm of turning herbs without conscious thought, when speaking to plant spirits feels less like performance and more like conversation with old friends. This is when belief stops being something you try to conjure and becomes something you simply *are*.

But here's what nobody mentions in the romantic versions: you'll doubt. You'll stand at your altar some random Tuesday feeling foolish, wondering if you're just talking to yourself, questioning whether any of this matters. Those moments aren't failures—they're the tradition testing whether you're serious. The ancestors watch not for unwavering certainty but for whether you show up anyway, whether you tend the relationship even when the evidence feels thin.

Faith deepens through accumulated evidence, not borrowed confidence. Each small result—the protection that held when you needed it, the healing tea that worked when nothing else did, the ancestor dream that answered your question—becomes a foundation stone. You're building something that will support you for decades, but only if you're willing to feel uncertain while the construction happens.

What comes next isn't more secrets to collect or advanced techniques to master. The deeper work involves integration: allowing these practices to reshape how you move through the world entirely. When you stop performing folk magic and start inhabiting a worldview where every threshold carries spiritual significance, where reciprocity governs all exchange, where the invisible world becomes as real as the visible one. That shift doesn't announce itself dramatically—it arrives quietly, in moments when you realize you've been leaving offerings without thinking about it, that you're asking permission before harvesting without conscious effort, that your faith has become woven into your daily rhythm so completely you can't separate magic from living.

The tradition survives not through those who learn it perfectly but through those who practice it faithfully.

Your grandmother didn't wait until her doubt disappeared before mixing her remedies. Your great-aunt didn't postpone protective work until her belief felt strong enough. They showed up with whatever faith they had that morning and let the work itself strengthen what needed strengthening.

So the question isn't whether you're ready. You're as ready now as you'll ever be, which is to say: partially prepared, somewhat uncertain, and standing at the threshold anyway. The mountain wisdom doesn't ask for more than that. It asks only whether you'll walk through that threshold and keep walking, one deliberate step after another, building faith through faithful practice until the path and the practitioner become indistinguishable.

Afterword

When you first opened these pages, perhaps the whispers of the Appalachian mountains called to you, promising secrets yet cloaked in mist. You sought to understand a magic that felt ancient, profound, and perhaps, just beyond your grasp. You might have felt a yearning for deeper connection, a desire to weave the unseen into the tapestry of your everyday, wondering how faith could truly intertwine with charm, how the earth could speak, and how ancestors could guide. You arrived, perhaps, with curiosity about old ways, or a longing to unearth a spiritual heritage that felt lost in the clamor of the modern world. Now, as this journey through the shadowed hollows and sun-drenched peaks of Appalachian folk magic draws to its close, you carry not just knowledge, but a deep, resonant understanding of the living current that runs through these hills and through your own spirit. You are no longer merely a seeker of secrets, but a nascent keeper of traditions, equipped with the wisdom to walk a path of profound connection and empowered practice.

We have walked the winding paths of tradition together, unearthing the profound truth that Appalachian folk magic is not a mere collection of spells or dusty incantations, but a vibrant, breathing faith. It is a tapestry woven from the sturdy threads of Celtic mysticism, the deep reverence of Indigenous wisdom, and the enduring hope of Christian devotion, all blended in the crucible of mountain isolation and necessity. We've learned that unwavering belief is the very cornerstone, the silent amplifier for every intention you set, transforming simple words into potent power. You've come to know the whispering counsel of ancestors and the ancient spirits of the land, discovering how to forge bonds of reciprocal respect that empower your every step and ground your spirit in the deep earth.

We delved into the sacred art of wildcrafting, learning to commune with plants as conscious allies, gathering medicine not just for the body, but for the soul, with gratitude and reverence as our compass. Then, we understood how to weave powerful protection, not through fear, but through layered intention, material intelligence, and ancestral strength, creating spiritual bulwarks against unseen tides. You learned the profound secrets of folk healing, where focused intention imbues plant wisdom with transformative power, distinguishing mere remedy from true spiritual medicine that touches the very core of being. And finally, we explored how to root your personal practice within the sacred rhythms of the mountains, finding the divine in the turning seasons, the quiet grace of your own altar, and the sacred dialogue of daily prayer.

This journey has revealed that authenticity and sincere reverence for the roots of this tradition are paramount, for without them, magic becomes mere mimicry. Consider, now, your life, attuned to the subtle currents of the wild, flowing with the sacred rhythm of the seasons, forever changed by the wisdom you've embraced. No longer will you feel adrift or disconnected, but anchored, knowing that the earth itself is a sanctuary, and your ancestors a constant guard, their presence a palpable comfort. Envision stepping into your own kitchen to prepare a simple meal, yet with every stir, every ingredient, you're infusing it with purpose, a blessing for health and hearth, a ritual of daily devotion. Your home, once just a dwelling, becomes a living altar, each threshold a place of layered protection, each corner imbued with intentional peace.

You won't simply walk through the woods; you'll stride through a cathedral, sensing the energetic wisdom of every fern, every ancient oak, feeling their conscious presence, their willingness to share their potent magic. The anxieties that once clung to you may now fall away, replaced by a deep-seated knowing that you are capable, protected, and connected to forces far greater than yourself. This isn't merely about doing magic; it's about becoming magic, about embodying a reverence for life that transforms every breath into a prayer, every action into a sacred ritual, every choice into a deliberate act of faith. You become a conduit, a keeper of the old ways, a living testament to the enduring power of faith and the wild, spiritual heart of the mountains.

Before these pages close and you step back into your ordinary world, let us perform one final, crucial act of magic: choose one specific secret from these pages, one that has resonated deepest within your soul, and commit to acting upon it before the day is done. Perhaps it is the crafting of a small protection sachet with herbs from your garden, speaking aloud your clear intention for safety and peace. Or perhaps it's the setting up of a simple altar corner, placing a smooth river stone and a photograph of an ancestor, and offering a silent prayer of gratitude. It might be to take a short, intentional walk in nature, asking permission from a plant before gathering a single fallen leaf, and leaving a small offering of cornmeal. Take ten minutes, just ten, to perform this single act with unwavering faith and focused presence. This isn't about perfectly executing a ritual; it's about the conscious, deliberate act of beginning, of planting the first seed of your ongoing practice.

It is in these small, consistent moments, repeated with sincerity, that the true, potent power of Appalachian folk magic takes root, growing from intention into tangible, lived reality. Let your conviction be the fuel, and your actions the tinder, igniting the sacred flame of your own rooted practice. Understand this, dear seeker: the path of mountain magic is not a race for perfection, nor is it a test of your flawless execution. There will be days when doubt clouds your vision, when distractions pull at your resolve, or when a ritual feels clumsy and ineffective in your hands. This is not failure; this is the human journey, and it is an intrinsic part of the work.

Remember, authenticity, humility, and consistent effort outweigh grand gestures and flashy results. You don't need to master every secret at once, nor must every working be a dramatic, immediate success. Instead, cultivate patience with yourself, offering the same gentle understanding you would to a fledgling sapling pushing through rocky soil, or a hesitant stream finding its way through the stones. Each small step, each whispered prayer, each conscious offering builds upon the last, creating a spiritual momentum that will carry you forward through seasons of plenty and seasons of barrenness.

You already possess the inherent wisdom, the spiritual hunger, and the profound capacity for connection. The seeds of mountain wisdom have been planted deep within you; now, tend them with gentle hands, unwavering faith, and a believing heart. The magic isn't outside of you, waiting to be found; it stirs within your very spirit, waiting to be awakened. The mountains have given their secrets, not to be hoarded, but to be woven into the vibrant fabric of your own unfolding life, enriching it with power, purpose, and profound connection. You are not merely a student; you are a living vessel, a bridge between the ancient whispers of the past and the unfolding potential of the present.

Go forth, then, with courage and deep conviction, remembering always that the deepest truth lies not in what you acquire, but in what you cultivate within your spirit. The greatest magic of all is a life lived with unwavering faith, in sacred relationship with all that is seen and unseen, and in humble, enduring gratitude for the wild, spiritual heart that beats within us all, echoing the ancient rhythm of the mountains. As you continue on this path, let the lessons of the mountains guide you, their wisdom a constant companion. Embrace the journey with an open heart, knowing that each step you take is a step toward a deeper understanding of yourself and the world around you. The magic of the Appalachians is now a part of you, a living, breathing force that will continue to grow and evolve as you do. Carry it with you, nurture it, and let it illuminate your path as you walk forward into the future.

As you move forward, remember that the journey is as important as the destination. Each moment spent in reflection, each act of kindness, and each gesture of gratitude adds to the tapestry of your life, enriching it with meaning and depth. The mountains have taught you to listen, to observe, and to honor the sacred in the everyday. Let these lessons guide you as you navigate the complexities of life, finding beauty in simplicity and strength in vulnerability. The path of Appalachian folk magic is one of continuous learning and growth, a journey that invites you to explore the depths of your own soul and the vastness of the world around you. Embrace it with an open heart and a curious mind, knowing that the magic you seek is already within you, waiting to be discovered and shared with the world.

Bibliography

Abramson, R., & Speer, J. H. (Eds.). (2006). <em>The Encyclopedia of Appalachia</em>. University of Tennessee Press.

Appalachian Forest Farmer Coalition. (2023, April 10). <i>The heart of holistic herbalism in Appalachia</i>. Southern Research Station. Retrieved from [URL where found if not already provided]

Association of Independent Readers and Rootworkers. (n.d.). The Book of Psalms in Folk Magic. Retrieved from

Blankenship, H. (2025, March 17). *Spring Cleaning: Appalachian Folk Magic Style*. Patheos. https://www.patheos.com/blogs/heatherblankenship/2025/03/17/spring-cleaning-appalachian-folk-magic-style/

Blue Ridge Tales. (2025, December 20). <i>Mountain Medicine: Remedies of the Granny Women</i>. https://blueridgetales.com/mountain-medicine-remedies-of-the-granny-women/

Johnson, C. P. E. (2013). <i>A Primer of Appalachian Magic: Working the Root, Crafting the Charm, and Conjuring the Spirit</i>. Weiser Books.

Canadian Conservation Institute. (2025, February 10). *Understanding how silver objects tarnish*. Canada.ca. https://www.canada.ca/en/conservation-institute/services/conservation-preservation-publications/cci-notes/understanding-silver-objects-tarnish.html

Cavender, A. (2003). <em>Folk Medicine in Southern Appalachia</em>. University of North Carolina Press.

Cavender, A. (2003). <em>Folk medicine in Southern Appalachia</em>. University of North Carolina Press.

Cavender, D. (2003). <i>A History of Appalachian Herbal Medicine</i>. McFarland & Company.

Chireau, Y. P. (2003). <em>Black Magic: Religion and the African American Conjuring Tradition</em>. University of California Press.

Confinity. (2024, January 27). *Samhain: A Time to Remember and Celebrate Ancestors*. Retrieved from https://confinity.io/blog/samhain-a-time-to-remember-and-celebrate-ancestors/

Conley, R. J. (2007). <i>A Cherokee Encyclopedia</i>. University of New Mexico Press.

Crews, J. (2010). Folklore, history, and ethnography in the Appalachian Mountains: An annotated bibliography. <em>Journal of Appalachian Studies</em>, <em>16</em> (1), 80-103.

Cunningham, S. (1985). <em>Cunningham's Encyclopedia of Magical Herbs</em>. Llewellyn Worldwide.

Evans, D. J. (2019). Granny Women, Mountain Root Doctors, and Traditional Appalachian Healing: A Historical and Cultural Perspective. <i>Appalachian Journal</i>, <i>46</i>(1/2), 100-125.

Danalis, F. (2019, November 11). *3 Reasons Why Your Intentions Aren't Materializing (and What To Do Instead)*. Felina Danalis | Somatic Experiencing & Coaching. Retrieved from https://felinadanalis.com/blog/3-reasons-why-your-intentions-arent-materializing-and-what-to-do-instead

Healthmantra. (n.d.). *12 Reasons Why Manifestation Practices Fail*. Retrieved from https://www.healthmantra.com/blog/12-reasons-why-manifestation-practices-fail

Morrison, D. (2018, March 7). *Reciprocity: A Witch's Relationship With Her Deities*. Patheos. Retrieved from https://www.patheos.com/blogs/between-the-shadows/2018/03/reciprocity-a-witchs-relationship-with-her-deities

Rankin, L. (2019, December 23). *Sacred Reciprocity: The Indigenous Spiritual Principle Of Giving & Receiving*. Lissa Rankin. Retrieved from https://lissarankin.com/ayni-sacred-reciprocity-indigenous-spiritual-principle-giving-receiving

Cailleachs Herbarium. (2016, May 28). *Folk magic and witchcraft | What's the difference*. Retrieved from https://cailleachsherbarium.com/2016/05/folk-magic-and-witchcraft-whats-the-difference

Davies, O. (2003). <i>Popular Magic: Cunning-Folk in English History</i>. Hambledon Continuum.

De Snoo, G. J., & Van der Linden, H. A. (1999). Foraging behaviour of European hares (Lepus europaeus) in the vicinity of a former zinc smelter: Consequences for lead and cadmium exposure. <em>Environmental Pollution</em>, <em>104</em>(1), 127–134.

Duke, J. A. (2002). <i>Handbook of Medicinal Herbs</i> (2nd ed.). CRC Press.

Echoes of Appalachia. (2026, April 17). <em>Appalachian Folklore Between History and Mystery</em>. Echoes of Appalachia. https://echoesofappalachia.com/appalachian-folklore-between-history-and-mystery/

Eclectic Herb. (2024, June 19). *Spotlight on St. John's Wort | Health Benefits*. Retrieved from https://www.eclecticherb.com/blogs/news/spotlight-on-st-johns-wort

Ghorbani, A., Esmaeilizadeh, M., Shahbazian, S., Rahimi, S., & Mohammadi, A. (2017). A systematic review on pharmacological properties of Achillea millefolium L. with emphasis on its wound healing effects. <i>Journal of Clinical and Diagnostic Research</i>, <i>11</i>(11), FE01–FE07.

Gieser, S. (2020). Ancestors and the Spiritual Practice of Creating Altars. <i>Journal of Transpersonal Psychology</i>.

Grove and Grotto. (2017, July 5). *Magickal symbols of protection*. https://www.groveandgrotto.com/blogs/articles/magickal-symbols-of-protection

Hag Stone Journal. (2019, November 22). <i>Appalachian Folk Magic: Healing, Death and Planting by the Signs</i>. Hag Stone Journal. Retrieved from [Insert URL if available]

Hamel, P. B., & Chiltoskey, M. U. (1975). <i>Cherokee Plants and Their Uses—A 400 Year History</i>. Herald Publishing Company.

Hand, W. D. (1980). <em>Magical Medicine: The Folk Healer</em>. University of California Press.

Hatfield, G. (2004). <i>Herbalists and Herbalism</i>. Dartmoor National Park Authority. Retrieved from https://www.dartmoor.gov.uk/__data/assets/pdf_file/0008/104597/traditional-medicinal-plants.pdf

Hoplon Designs. (2026, April 1). *Brauche: The Secret Folk Magic of PA*. Retrieved from https://hoplon-designs.com/blogs/news/brauche-the-secret-folk-magic-of-pa

Hubbs, N. (2023). <i>Folklore and History of the Domovoi (House Spirit)</i>. Mythology & Folklore. Retrieved from https://mythologyandfolklore.com/folklore/domovoi/

Keville, K. (2016). <i>The Illustrated Herb Encyclopedia: A Complete Culinary, Medicinal, Cosmetic, and Aromatic Guide to Over 100 Herbs</i>. Sterling Publishing Co., Inc.

Kimball, J. (2025, February 28). <i>The Bible as a Spellbook: Folk Magic and Cultural Beliefs in Southern Appalachia</i>. jess kimball. https://jesskimball.substack.com/p/the-bible-as-a-spellbook-folk-magic

Koziol, M. (2020, June 29). *Do You Stir Clockwise?* Silver Owl Tarot. https://silverowltarot.com/do-you-stir-clockwise/

Kregiel, D., Pawlikowska, E., & Antolak, H. (2018). Urtica dioica L. (stinging nettle): A source of biologically active compounds. In <i>Herbal Medicine</i>. IntechOpen. https://www.intechopen.com/chapters/60784

Kriebel, D. W. (2007). *Powwowing Among the Pennsylvania Dutch: A Traditional Medical Practice in the Modern World*. Penn State University Press.

Stone, L. L. (2018). <i>The Cultural and Historical Context of Appalachian Folk Magic</i>. University Press of Kentucky.

Leopold, S. (2026, February 16). *Conservation Challenges & Ecological Importance*. Herbal Reality. https://www.herbalreality.com/conservation-challenges-ecological-importance/

Ramirez, R. (2022, April 1). *How the Rage for Sage Threatens Native American Traditions and Recipes*. Atlas Obscura. https://www.atlasobscura.com/articles/white-sage-smudging-native-american-appropriation

Pember, M. A. (2019, May 29). *Native Americans Troubled By The Appropriation And Commoditization Of Smudging*. Beauty Independent. https://www.beautyindependent.com/native-americans-troubled-appropriation-commoditization-smudging/

California State University Long Beach. (2022, April 28). *Ecological Damage on White Sage*. https://www.csulb.edu/division-student-affairs/news/ecological-damage-white-sage

Lewis, M., & Lewis, J. (2018). The Practice of Ancestor Veneration: Sacred Spaces and Rituals. <i>Sacred Spaces: A Journal of Religion and Culture</i>, <i>1</i>(1), 34-48.

Libretexts. (2023, March 10). *Lattices and Unit Cells of Salt*. Chemistry LibreTexts. https://chem.libretexts.org/Bookshelves/Physical_and_Theoretical_Chemistry_Textbook_Maps/Supplemental_Modules_(Physical_and_Theoretical_Chemistry)/Chemical_Bonding/Intermolecular_Forces/Crystalline_Solids/Lattices_and_Unit_Cells_of_S

Long, J. M. (2012). <em>The Book of Psalms in American Folk and Hoodoo Traditions</em>. University Press of Mississippi.

MacNeill, M. (2008). <i>The Festival of Lughnasa: A Study of the Survival of the Celtic Festival of the Beginning of Harvest</i>. Oxford University Press.

Malhotra, P. A. (2021). Cultural and Spiritual Significance of Sage and Smudging in Indigenous Traditions. <em>Journal of Indigenous Spirituality and Cultural Practices</em>, <em>5</em>(2), 45-58.

Mason, R. (2023). <em>Spirit & lore: The practical guide to conjure, rootwork & folk magic</em>. Weiser Books.

McCauley, D. R. (2007). <i>Appalachian Folk Religion: A Source Book</i>. University Press of Kentucky.

Meadowlark Motel. (2021, April 5). <em>Pagan Traditions and Granny Magic in the Great Smoky Mountains</em>. Meadowlark Motel. https://meadowlarkmotel.com/pagan-traditions-and-granny-magic-in-the-great-smoky-mountains/

Milnes, G. (2025, April 14). <i>Bibles, Roots, and Spirits: The Secret Magic of Southern, Appalachian and Native American Faith</i>. The Folklorist. https://thefolklorist.substack.com/p/bibles-roots-and-spirits-the-secret

Milnes, G. C. (2007). <i>Signs, Cures, & Witchery: German Appalachian Folklore</i>. University of Tennessee Press.

Mississippi State University. (2025, July 9). <i>Traveling Jack: Tracing Settler Identity Through Appalachian Folklore - Scholars Junction</i>. Scholars Junction. Retrieved from [Insert URL if available]

Mooney, J. (1900). <i>Myths of the Cherokee</i>. Bureau of American Ethnology, Nineteenth Annual Report, 1897–98, Part 1, 1–548.

Neely, K. H. (2020, April 18). *THE LEGEND OF THE FAIRY CROSS*. Kirk H. Neely (Blog). https://kirkneely.com/the-legend-of-the-fairy-cross/

Paluch, E., Zizio, S., Kordali, S., Koç, M., Topuz, M., Çelik, M. M., Çelik, A., Çobanoğlu, E., & Ganjali, M. R. (2021). Ruta Essential Oils: Composition and Bioactivities. *Molecules*, *26*(12), 3742.

Patheos. (2019, June 11). <i>Backwoods Witchcraft: Appalachian Folk Magic | Guest Contributor</i>. Patheos. Retrieved from [Insert URL if available]

Pavlina, S. (2006, May 29). *Why Do Intentions Take So Long to Manifest?*. Retrieved from https://www.stevepavlina.com/blog/2006/05/why-do-intentions-take-so-long-to-manifest

Healthmantra. (n.d.). *12 Reasons Why Manifestation Practices Fail*. Retrieved from https://www.healthmantra.com/blog/12-reasons-why-manifestation-practices-fail

Danalis, D. (2025, December 25). *Why Your Manifestations Aren't Working*. The Human Lens | Medium. Retrieved from https://medium.com/the-human-lens/why-your-manifestations-arent-working-6671408139d4

Haseman, M. (2018, January 22). *How to Set a Magickal Intention*. Mumbles & Things. Retrieved from https://www.mumblesandthings.com/blog/how-to-set-a-magickal-intention

Mankey, J. (2017, November 28). *The Secret To Witchcraft & Magick Is Intent*. Patheos. Retrieved from https://www.patheos.com/blogs/panmankey/2017/11/secret-witchcraft-magick-intent

Penczak, C. (2019). <em>The mighty dead: An introduction to ancestor worship</em>. Llewellyn Publications.

Raboteau, A. J. (2004). <em>Slave religion: The 'invisible institution' in the antebellum South</em>. Oxford University Press.

<i>Red Thread: The Folklore of Protection and Healing</i>. (2023). Mythology & Folklore. Retrieved from https://mythologyandfolklore.com/red-thread-the-folklore-of-protection-and-healing/

Richards, J. (2021). <i>Servant of the Spirits: Appalachian Conjure & the Roots of Hoodoo</i>. Weiser Books.

Richards, J. (2022, February 6). <em>Appalachian Folk Magic and Christianity</em>.

Scribd. https://www.scribd.com/document/556942691/Appalachian-Folk-Magic-and-Christianity

Riggs, A. (2018). <i>A Primer on the Cherokee Language: A Resource for Teachers and Learners</i>. University of North Carolina Press.

RiverWind, J., & RiverWind, L. (2021). A Prophecy Fulfilled. The Vineyard JC. Retrieved from

Kimmerer, R. W. (2017, March 2). <i>The Teachings of Plants: Finding Common Ground Between Traditional and Scientific Knowledge</i>. YouTube. Retrieved from https://www.youtube.com/watch?v=LdYtIq4x7y8; Thane, J. G., Warner, K., Webb, S. R., & Burgess, R. (2021, November 10). <i>Ethnobotany—The Intersection of Plants, People, and Culture: 'Our Common Ground' Conversation Recap</i>. Marin Agricultural Land Trust. Retrieved from https://www.malt.org/ethnobotany-the-intersection-of-plants-people-and-culture-our-common-ground-conversation-recap/; Calvo, P., Gagliano, M., Souza, G. M., & Trewavas, A. (2020, November 16). Debunking a myth: plant consciousness. <i>Plants</i>, <i>9</i>(11), 1571. doi:10.3390/plants9111571; The Wellness Practitioner. (2025, June 15). <i>The Spirit of Plants: Plant Consciousness & Communication</i>. The Wellness Practitioner. Retrieved from https://thewellnesspractitioner.com/the-spirit-of-plants-plant-consciousness-communication/

Saad, B., & Said, O. (2011). <i>Traditional Arabic Medicine</i>. Wiley-Blackwell.

Smith, T. J. (2015). Conjure and Cure: A Folkloric Study of Traditional Healing Practices in Southern Appalachia. <i>Journal of Appalachian Studies</i>, <i>21</i>(1), 80-97.

Tame the Spirit Herbs. (n.d.). <i>Yellow Root - Appalachian Mountains Wild Harvest</i>. Retrieved from https://www.tamethespiritherbs.com/product/yellow-root-appalachian-mountains-wild-harvest/; Gardening and Ethnobotany in Academia Project. (n.d.). <i>Yellowroot</i>. Retrieved from https://ethnobotany.ku.edu/plants/yellowroot; Chestnut School of Herbal Medicine. (2026, March 23). <i>Yellowroot (Xanthorhiza simplicissima)</i>. Retrieved from https://chestnutherbs.com/yellowroot-xanthorhiza-simplicissima/; Colenbaugh, C. (2021, June 19). <i>Natural and Cultural History of Xanthorhiza simplicissima</i>. ResearchGate. Retrieved from https://www.researchgate.net/publication/352528751_Natural_and_Cultural_History_of_Xanthorhiza_simplicissima

Telesco, P. (2020). <em>A Witch's Guide to Lunar Magic: The Complete Guide to Moon Magic, Spells, and Rituals for All 8 Phases of the Moon</em>. Llewellyn Worldwide.

The Editors of Encyclopaedia Britannica. (2024). <i>Sādhanā</i>. Encyclopaedia Britannica. Retrieved from https://www.britannica.com/topic/sadhanas

The House of Ashé. (n.d.). <i>Devil's Shoestring, Whole</i>. Retrieved from https://thehouseofashe.com/products/devils-shoestring-whole; Wax Spiritual. (n.d.). <i>Devil's Shoestring</i>. Retrieved from https://waxspiritual.com/products/devils-shoestring; Yeyeo Botanica. (n.d.). <i>Devil's Shoestring</i>. Retrieved from https://www.yeyeobotanica.com/products/devils-shoestring; Conjured Cardea. (n.d.). <i>Devil's Shoestring Roots-Trip up the Devil,Protection,Clear Evil</i>. Retrieved from https://conjuredcardea.com/products/devils-shoestring-roots-trip-up-the-devil-protection-clear-evil; Rasbold, K. (2024, November 25). <i>Herbalism For Your Day: Rue</i>. Green Egg Magazine. Retrieved from https://greeneggmagazine.com/herbal

ism-for-your-day-rue/; Original Botanica. (2023, January 24). <i>The Magical Uses of the Rue Plant | Protection, Luck, Money</i>. Retrieved from https://originalbotanica.com/blog/magical-uses-rue-plant-protection-luck-money/; Goddess Elite. (2023, November 14). <i>Rue: Unveiling its Magical Uses</i>. Retrieved from https://goddesselite.com/blogs/news/rue-unveiling-its-magical-uses; The Steampunk Buddha. (2026, January 22). <i>Rue: The Classic Protection & Psychic Herb</i>. Retrieved from https://thesteampunkbuddha.com/blogs/blog/rue-the-classic-protection-psychic-herb; the eleventh house. (2023, October 30). <i>Plant & Crystal Magic 32: Rue & Orange Calcite</i>. Retrieved from https://theeleventhhouse.co/blogs/the-eleventh-house-blog/plant-crystal-magic-32-rue-orange-calcite

The Wilderness Society. (n.d.). *When to Go: Southern Appalachians*. Retrieved from https://www.wilderness.org/articles/article/when-go-southern-appalachians

Tinker, G. E. (2004). Sacred land: the spiritual significance of the land to American Indians. <i>Environmental Ethics</i>, <i>26</i>(3), 271-285.

Tinker, G. E. (2004). <i>Spirit and resistance: political theology and American Indian liberation</i>. Fortress Press.

Turker, A. U., & Gurel, E. (2005). Common mullein (Verbascum thapsus L.): historical uses, phytochemistry and biotechnology. <i>Journal of Ethnopharmacology</i>, <i>96</i>(3), 407-416.

Turley, J. (2026, April 11). *Ramps: The Pungent Pride of Appalachian Spring*. Medium. Retrieved from https://medium.com/@john.turley.nc/ramps-the-pungent-pride-of-appalachian-spring-108719d3f112

Volkov, A. G. (2012). <i>Plant electrophysiology: Signaling and responses</i>. Springer Science & Business Media.

Wigginton, E. (1972). <em>The Foxfire Book</em>. Anchor Books.

Wildfoods 4 Wildlife. (n.d.). *Foraging ethics*. Retrieved from https://wildfoods4wildlife.org/foraging-ethics/

Boye, K. (2024, April 25). *What is wildcrafting? Responsible harvesting from the wild*. Organic India. https://organicindiausa.com/blog/what-is-wildcrafting/

Yoga Journal. (2021). <i>Sadhana: A Daily Spiritual Practice</i>. Retrieved from https://www.yogajournal.com/yoga-101/sadhana-a-daily-spiritual-practice/

Yronwode, C. (2002). <i>Hoodoo Herb and Root Dictionary</i>. Lucky Mojo Curio Co. Retrieved from https://www.luckymojo.com/psalms.html

Yun, H., & Lee, S. M. (2018). Ginseng: A botanical drug for the treatment of various disorders. <i>Journal of Ginseng Research</i>, <i>42</i>(2), 129–131. https://doi.org/10.1016/j.jgr.2017.02.004

aromaG's Botanica. (2021, October 10). *Appalachian Folk Magic – Protection from Ghosts & Ghouls*. https://www.aromagsbotanica.com/blogs/news/appalachian-folk-magic-protection-from-ghosts-ghouls

www.ingramcontent.com/pod-product-compliance
Lightning Source LLC
LaVergne TN
LVHW010933110826
845149LV00013B/2579